FROM STRESS

Success

Eigh... ...ieving
...ness

ELEANOR BLANCHE

Eleanor Blanche© Copyright 2025 - All rights reserved.

The content contained within this book may not be reproduced, duplicated or transmitted without direct written permission from the author or the publisher.

Under no circumstances will any blame or legal responsibility be held against the publisher, or author, for any damages, reparation, or monetary loss due to the information contained within this book, either directly or indirectly.

Legal Notice:

This book is copyright protected. It is only for personal use. You cannot amend, distribute, sell, use, quote or paraphrase any part, or the content within this book, without the consent of the author or publisher.

Disclaimer Notice:

Please note the information contained within this document is for educational and entertainment purposes only. All effort has been executed to present accurate, up to date, reliable, complete information. No warranties of any kind are declared or implied. Readers acknowledge that the author is not engaged in the rendering of legal, financial, medical or professional advice. The content within this book has been derived from various sources. Please consult a licensed professional before attempting any techniques outlined in this book.

By reading this document, the reader agrees that under no circumstances is the author responsible for any losses, direct or indirect, that are incurred as a result of the use of the information contained within this document, including, but not limited to, errors, omissions, or inaccuracies.

Table of Contents

A NOTE FROM THE AUTHOR 1

INTRODUCTION 3

CHAPTER 1: UNDERSTANDING STRESS AND ITS IMPACT 7

What Happens to Your Body Under Stress? 8
  Spotting the Physical Signs of Stress 8

CHAPTER 2: BREAKING THE HABITS OF OVERTHINKING 19

Common Triggers of Overthinking 20
  Practical Ways to Worry Less 23
  Practical Exercises to Stop Overthinking 23

CHAPTER 3: CREATING SPACE BETWEEN YOU AND YOUR THOUGHTS 31

The Power of Labelling and Observing Thoughts 32
  The Long-Term Benefits 35

CHAPTER 4: CULTIVATING SELF-COMPASSION 41

Benefits of Self-Compassion 41
  Simple Ways to Nurture Self-Kindness 43

CHAPTER 5: CONNECTING TO THE PRESENT MOMENT 51

How Mindfulness Helps You Tune Into the Present 52
  Body Awareness 52
  Body Scanning 52
  Mindful Breathing 53

CHAPTER 6: OBSERVING WITHOUT JUDGEMENT 67

The Nature of Judgment 68
  Transforming Stressful Moments Through Observation 70
  How to Cultivate Nonjudgmental Awareness 70
  How These Techniques Work Together 73

CHAPTER 7: DEVELOPING EMOTIONAL AWARENESS 77

The Connection Between Thoughts and Emotions 78
  How Mindfulness Improves Emotional Awareness 79
  Investigate: Explore with Curiosity 84

CHAPTER 8: SUSTAINING MINDFULNESS IN EVERYDAY LIFE 93

CONCLUSION 98

GLOSSARY 101

REFERENCES **106**

A Note from the Author

Peace comes from within. Do not seek it without. –Buddha

This little book is designed to provide you with simple yet powerful tips for experiencing the present moment through daily mindful practice. We live in a world where there seems to be no end to the external challenges that invade our daily lives. I will show you how to take a step back and savor the present moment by using basic techniques for mindful awareness. I hope you enjoy this journey with me.

Introduction

What if you woke up in the middle of the night, gasping—not because you couldn't breathe, but because the weight of stress and anxiety felt suffocating? For years, I lived in this exhausting cycle. I was running on empty, surviving on barely four hours of sleep a night.

Work deadlines loomed over me, personal responsibilities piled up, and no matter how hard I tried, I always felt like I was falling behind. The things I once cared about—my job, my relationships, even my well-being—started to feel like burdens. Sleep became a luxury, while exhaustion became my norm.

If you've ever felt like I did, then you're familiar with the constant barrage of demands and distractions we face today. They can leave us feeling overwhelmed, disconnected, and out of sync with ourselves. Our minds race from worry to worry, and our bodies remain tense.

But there is a way to break free from this mental clutter. It's possible to find peace not in some distant future but in the very moment you're living in right now.

This book is designed to help you do just that. *From Stress to Stillness* will guide you through a transformative journey—one step at a time—from the chaos of negative thinking to the calm of mindful awareness. It will be a gradual unfolding of your ability to be present, peaceful, and more connected with yourself and the world around you.

That's what mindfulness is all about—being aware of your thoughts, feelings, and physical sensations without judgment or attachment. It's a simple yet profound practice that can change the way you experience life, helping you break free from the grip of stress and negative thinking.

In this book, you will learn eight essential steps that will take you from a place of mental and emotional overwhelm to a state of mindfulness and presence. Why eight steps? The number eight symbolizes balance, renewal, and infinite possibility. Many ancient traditions, including Buddhism's Eightfold Path, emphasize structured steps toward enlightenment and inner harmony. In this book, you will follow a modern, practical approach to achieving mindfulness—one step at a time.

Each chapter introduces a new stage of the journey, from recognizing the signs of stress to creating space between yourself and your thoughts, cultivating self-compassion, and ultimately learning to live mindfully in your everyday life.

Along the way, I will share practical techniques, exercises, and real-life stories to guide you in applying mindfulness to your own experiences. Are you new to mindfulness, or have you been practicing for some time? These steps will help you deepen your awareness, transform your relationship with your thoughts, and cultivate lasting peace.

This journey won't always be easy, but it will be worthwhile. You will learn to approach circumstances with clarity, compassion, and an open heart. As you progress through this book, you will find that the stress and negativity you once felt trapped by can gradually loosen their hold as you regain a sense of stillness and well-being.

Are you ready to begin? The first step is simply recognizing where you are right now—and with that, you have already begun your journey.

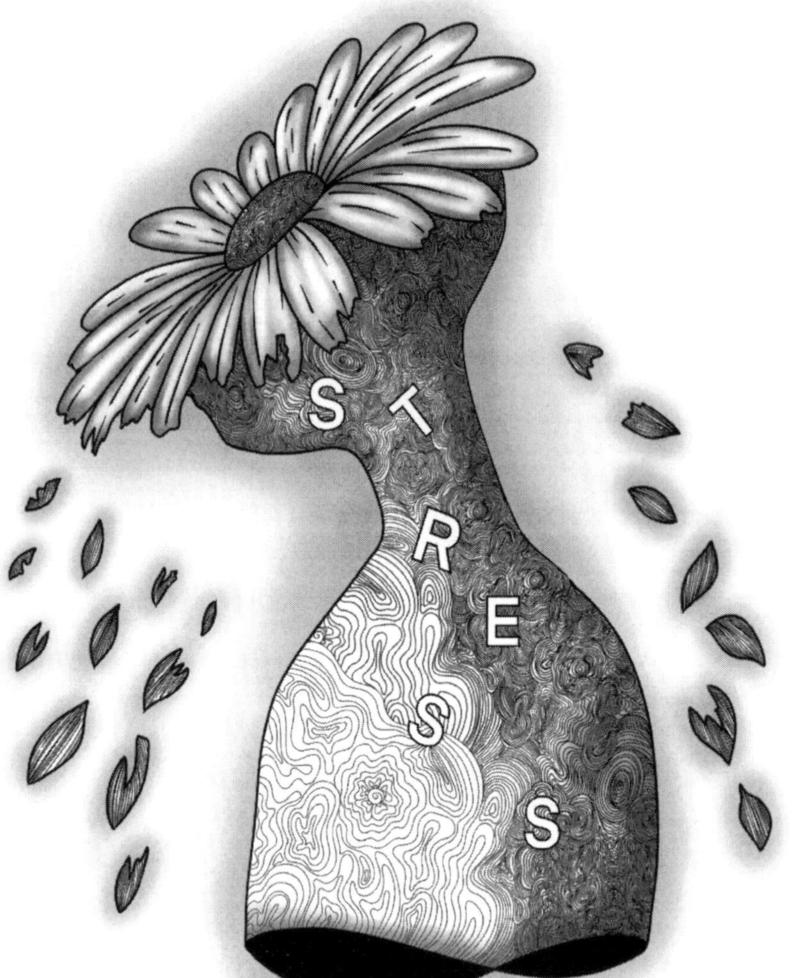
STRESS

Chapter 1

Understanding Stress

and Its Impact

There is no path to peace. Peace is the path. –Mahatma Gandhi

Stress is a natural and often unavoidable part of life. It is our body's response to perceived threats, challenges, or demands—whether physical, emotional, or psychological. However, it is not always negative. A little bit of stress, scientifically referred to as eustress, can motivate us to perform better and rise to challenges. This could manifest as a feeling of excitement before a big presentation or an adrenaline rush during a competition.

On the flip side, when stress becomes overwhelming and life feels like a never-ending to-do list with no break in sight, it can turn into distress. This type of stress can drain our energy, disrupt our emotions, and negatively affect our health.

What Happens to Your Body Under Stress?

When your brain perceives a threat, even if it's just an overflowing inbox, it signals the adrenal glands to release stress hormones such as cortisol and adrenaline. This triggers the classic "fight or flight" response—your heart races, your muscles tense up, and your body prepares to tackle or escape the problem.

Your autonomic nervous system (ANS) plays a significant role here. The sympathetic nervous system (SNS) prepares you to react, while the parasympathetic nervous system (PNS) helps you calm down once the danger has passed.

However, if stress persists for too long, it can disrupt your body's balance. Your hypothalamic-pituitary-adrenal (HPA) axis, which we can simply refer to as the brain response system, remains activated, keeping cortisol levels elevated. This prolonged activation can lead to fatigue, weakened immunity, and even mental health issues.

Spotting the Physical Signs of Stress

The way we deal with stress doesn't always look or feel the same for everyone. Sometimes, it can sneak into our lives quietly, changing how we feel and function without our noticing. Often, the first signs of stress show up in our bodies—little aches, pains, or discomforts that might seem normal at first but are your body's way of communicating, saying, "Hey, something's not right here."

If we listen to them early on, we can stop stress from snowballing into bigger health problems later. Do these signs feel familiar? What might they be telling you about the stress you're carrying? But how does it build up?

It might start in the mind, and you may tolerate it for a while, but it eventually shows up in your body. That could be a headache that hits after a crazy day or the tightness in your shoulders that just won't go away.

At first, you might think that the back pain and migraines are a result of work or relationship pressure, causing you to brush it off. But over time, the pain intensifies. If we don't pay attention to these signs, they can turn into something much bigger, like chronic stress. If chronic stress is allowed to have a freeway, it can affect key parts of our bodies and impair their function:

Cardiovascular System

When you experience stress, your heart rate can increase, and your blood pressure may rise. This occurs because stress triggers the release of hormones that prepare your body for a fight-or-flight response. These hormones cause your heart to pump faster and constrict your blood vessels. Over time, this constant state of heightened alertness can increase the risk of serious health issues. For instance, high blood pressure, or hypertension, can develop due to long-term exposure to stress. Hypertension can lead to heart disease, which is one of the leading causes of death worldwide. Similarly, chronic stress can increase the risk of stroke, which occurs when blood flow to the brain is interrupted.

To counteract these effects, find stress-reducing techniques. Regular physical activity can help lower blood pressure and improve heart health. Even simple exercises such as walking or cycling can be beneficial. Additionally, practicing relaxation techniques like deep breathing, meditation, or yoga can help calm the mind and lower your heart rate.

Immune System

When the body is under constant stress, the immune system can become suppressed. The body becomes less capable of fighting off infections and diseases. For example, individuals experiencing prolonged stress may become more susceptible to the common cold or flu. Additionally, stress can slow down the healing process when one is injured or falls ill.

To maintain a strong immune system, practice regular exercise, eat a balanced diet rich in vitamins and minerals, and ensure you get adequate sleep. Engaging in social activities and fostering relationships can also provide emotional support, which can help mitigate stress. Seeking professional help, such as talking to a counselor or therapist, is another effective way to develop coping skills for managing stress better.

Gastrointestinal System

Stress can lead to or exacerbate existing gastrointestinal or digestive problems, such as irritable bowel syndrome (IBS), ulcers, and acid reflux. The connection between stress and the digestive system can be attributed to how the brain and gut communicate. When a person is stressed, the body prioritizes resources to deal with the stress instead of focusing on digestion, leading to various digestive issues.

This relationship implies that managing stress can also alleviate some gastrointestinal problems. Eating smaller, more frequent meals rather than large meals can aid digestion. Individuals can also incorporate fiber-rich foods, such as whole grains, fruits, and vegetables, which can promote better gut health. Additionally, it is helpful to pay attention to drinking enough water and to avoid excessive caffeine and alcohol, as these can worsen gastrointestinal symptoms.

Endocrine System

Stress can throw your hormones out of balance as well. Your endocrine system, which controls hormone levels in your body, takes a significant hit when stress becomes a regular part of life. When your hormones are out of sync, it can lead to various health issues. Suddenly, you may begin craving junk food, and that's cortisol at work. When stress levels remain elevated for too long, your body releases extra cortisol, a hormone that increases hunger and encourages fat storage—especially around the belly. This can lead to unhealthy eating habits, making weight gain even more likely.

Chronic stress can also interfere with your insulin sensitivity, making it harder for your body to regulate blood sugar. Over time, this can increase the risk of diabetes, as high blood sugar levels become more difficult to control.

Your thyroid, which helps regulate metabolism and energy levels, can also be affected by stress. When stress hormones interfere with thyroid function, you may feel fatigued, sluggish, or struggle with weight fluctuations.

To prevent such health complications, include regular physical activity in your routine. Exercise can help balance hormones naturally and promote a sense of well-being. Managing stress through mindfulness practices, such as meditation or journaling, can also help reestablish hormonal balance by reducing cortisol levels.

Musculoskeletal System

When we think about stress, we often picture a racing heart or an anxious mind, but did you know it can take a serious toll on your muscles as well? It can be as simple as experiencing a tension headache after a stressful day or noticing your shoulders creeping up to your ears without realizing it.

When you're under pressure, your body instinctively tightens up, almost as if it's bracing for impact. Over time, this constant muscle tension can lead to aches, stiffness, and even chronic pain.

So, what can you do? Movement is vital. Gentle stretching, yoga, or tai chi can help loosen those tight muscles and improve flexibility. Taking short breaks throughout the day—whether it's standing up to stretch, going for a quick walk, or just rolling your shoulders—can also make a significant difference. Even just 10 minutes a day of stretching or deep breathing can have a positive impact. And don't forget to rest! Your body needs downtime to recover. The more you practice, the better you'll become at spotting those stress signals early, and the more equipped you'll be to address them. In the latter chapters, we will discuss these practical aspects in detail.

How Stress Affects Your Mind and Behavior

As we've noted, stress alters the way your brain functions. For example, an individual may have trouble focusing when they feel overwhelmed. They might forget something important because their mind is racing. It can disrupt your attention, memory, daily habits, and even decision-making. Therefore, understanding how it impacts your mind and behavior can help you develop healthy coping strategies and maintain your mental well-being.

Let's see how:

- **Cognitive Appraisal:** How you think about stress matters. If you perceive a challenge as something you can handle, you're more likely to remain calm. However, if it feels overwhelming, stress can become unbearable.

- **Emotional Rollercoaster:** Stress can trigger feelings of frustration, anxiety, or even sadness. Over time, chronic stress can contribute to mood disorders, such as depression and anxiety.

- **Behavioral Changes:** Have you ever noticed how stress affects your eating and sleeping habits? Some people lose their appetite, while others crave comfort food. Some struggle to sleep, while others sleep excessively. Stress can also lead to coping mechanisms like avoidance, irritability, or even dependence on unhealthy substances.

Social and Occupational Impact

Stress also has broader social and occupational implications, which include the following:

- **Relationships:** It can strain personal relationships, leading to conflicts, communication breakdowns, and emotional distance.

- **Workplace:** In the workplace, stress can reduce productivity, increase absenteeism, and contribute to job dissatisfaction. It can also lead to burnout, a state of physical and emotional exhaustion.

- **Societal Costs:** The societal costs of stress are substantial, including healthcare expenses, lost productivity, and the impact on public health systems.

Negative Thoughts Fuel Stress and Anxiety

Have you ever noticed someone changing direction when they saw you coming and immediately thought, *Did I do something wrong? Am I that irritating to them?* Before you know it, your mind is spinning with self-doubt and worry.

These kinds of thoughts arise all the time, often without us even realizing it. But the problem isn't just the thought itself—it's what happens next. If we allow it to take hold, it can spiral into stress, anxiety, and self-criticism.

Our thoughts, emotions, and bodies are all connected—when we think negatively, we feel anxious, and our bodies respond with tension, a racing heart, or restlessness. Then, those physical symptoms make us even more stressed. It's a vicious cycle. This process can be understood through the interplay of cognitive, emotional, and physiological factors. Here's a detailed explanation:

Cognitive Appraisal and Negative Thinking

Maybe you made a small mistake at work and suddenly thought, *That's it. I'm going to get fired.* Or you struggled with one task and told yourself, *I always fail at everything.* These patterns of negative thinking can make daily challenges feel much bigger than they are—and that can send stress levels through the roof.

This happens because of cognitive appraisal—essentially, the way we interpret and evaluate situations. When our thoughts lean negative, we can end up distorting reality without even realizing it. Here are a few common traps:

- **Catastrophizing:** Expecting the absolute worst. A tiny mistake feels like a disaster, and suddenly, you're convinced everything is falling apart.

- **Overgeneralizing:** Letting one setback define everything. One failure? *That must mean I fail at everything.*

- **Black-and-White Thinking:** Seeing only extremes—either you're perfect, or you're a complete failure. These cognitive distortions can make situations seem more threatening than they are, triggering a stress response.

Emotional Responses

Negative thoughts can often lead to negative emotions, such as fear, sadness, and anger. These emotions can intensify the perception of stress and create a feedback loop.

- **Fear and Anxiety:** Negative thoughts can evoke fear and anxiety, which in turn can lead to more negative thoughts. For example, worrying about an upcoming presentation might lead to thoughts such as, "What if I mess up?" which increases anxiety.

- **Sadness and Depression:** Persistent negative thinking can contribute to feelings of hopelessness and sadness, which can exacerbate stress and lead to depressive symptoms.

- **Anger and Frustration:** Negative thoughts can also trigger anger and frustration, which can increase stress levels and lead to aggressive or avoidant behaviors.

Physiological Responses

Your body's stress response is closely linked to cognitive and emotional processes.

Negative thoughts can activate the sympathetic nervous system (SNS) and the hypothalamic-pituitary-adrenal (HPA) axis, leading to the release of stress hormones such as cortisol and adrenaline.

When negative thoughts are persistent, the stress response can become chronic, resulting in sustained high levels of stress hormones. This can have detrimental effects on physical health.

Behavioral Responses

Negative thoughts can shape actions in ways that intensify stress and anxiety. Here's how this occurs:

- **Avoidance:** Have you ever skipped a social event because you were worried about what people might think? Avoiding stressful situations might bring short-term relief, but in the long run, it can increase anxiety and make fears even harder to face.

- **Unhealthy Coping Strategies:** Stress can push people toward habits like overeating, binge-watching TV, or even relying on substances to numb their anxiety. While these may feel comforting in the moment, they don't solve the problem and can make stress worse over time.

- **Struggling to Solve Problems:** When stress levels are high, it's harder to think clearly and find solutions. This can leave you feeling stuck, overwhelmed, and even more anxious, reinforcing the cycle of negative thinking.

Dealing With Negative Thoughts

To get past these negative thought loops, recognize them for what they are—habitual patterns, not absolute truths. Once you do that, you can start shifting your mindset. Here's how:

1. **Challenge the Thought:** Ask yourself, *Is this true? What's the evidence for and against this belief?* If a friend were thinking this way, what would you tell them? Often, you'll realize these thoughts don't hold up under scrutiny.

2. **Reframe Your Thinking:** Instead of saying, "I always fail," try saying, "I've had successes and setbacks, and I can learn from both." Small shifts in language can make a big difference in how you see yourself.

3. **Use Positive Affirmations:** It might feel strange at first, but repeating affirmations such as, *I am capable* or *I am doing my best, and that is enough,* can help rewire your thought patterns over time.

4. **Practice Gratitude:** When negativity starts creeping in, shift your focus to what's going right. Jotting down just three things you're grateful for each day can train your brain to notice more of the good.

Breaking Free From Autopilot

Have you ever had a day when you went through all your usual routines—waking up, commuting, working, scrolling on your phone, and eating dinner—only to realize later that you barely remember any of it? When life starts to feel like a checklist of tasks rather than a series of meaningful experiences, you're in autopilot mode.

While routines can bring structure, they can also leave you feeling disconnected, drained, and trapped in a loop that only adds to your stress. However, you don't have to remain stuck in this loop. Simple techniques like mindfulness, deep breathing, or even challenging negative thoughts when they arise can help calm your body and shift your mindset. For example:

- **Engage Your Senses:** The next time you eat, actually taste your food. Notice the textures, the flavors, and the experience of eating rather than just consuming.

- **Change Up Your Routine:** Take a different route to work, listen to a new playlist, or try a new activity. Small changes force your brain to wake up and engage with the moment.

- **Healthy Lifestyle Choices:** Regular exercise, a balanced diet, adequate sleep, and mindfulness practices can help manage stress levels.

- **Social Support:** Strong social connections and support networks can provide emotional comfort and practical assistance during times of stress.

- **Cognitive-Behavioral Techniques:** Cognitive-behavioral therapy (CBT) and other psychological interventions can help individuals reframe negative thoughts and develop healthier coping strategies.

- **Time Management:** Effective time management and prioritization can reduce the feeling of being overwhelmed and help individuals regain a sense of control.

- **Practice Grounding Techniques:** Feel your feet on the floor. Notice the weight of your body in your chair. Take a deep breath and truly *feel* it. These tiny actions bring you back to the present.

- **Mindful Movement:** Whether it's yoga, stretching, or simply walking while paying attention to your surroundings, moving with awareness helps break the cycle of mindless routines.

***

Stress has a way of weaving itself into every corner of our lives—physically, mentally, and emotionally. We've seen how it manifests, often subtly at first, before building into something more overwhelming. More importantly, we've discovered that stress doesn't have to dictate our lives.

Through awareness, mindful practices, and proactive self-care, we can break free from its grip. This can be achieved through small habits such as cognitive restructuring or simply stepping out of our routine to engage with the present moment. In the next chapter, we will explore how we can break free from one of its habits: overthinking.

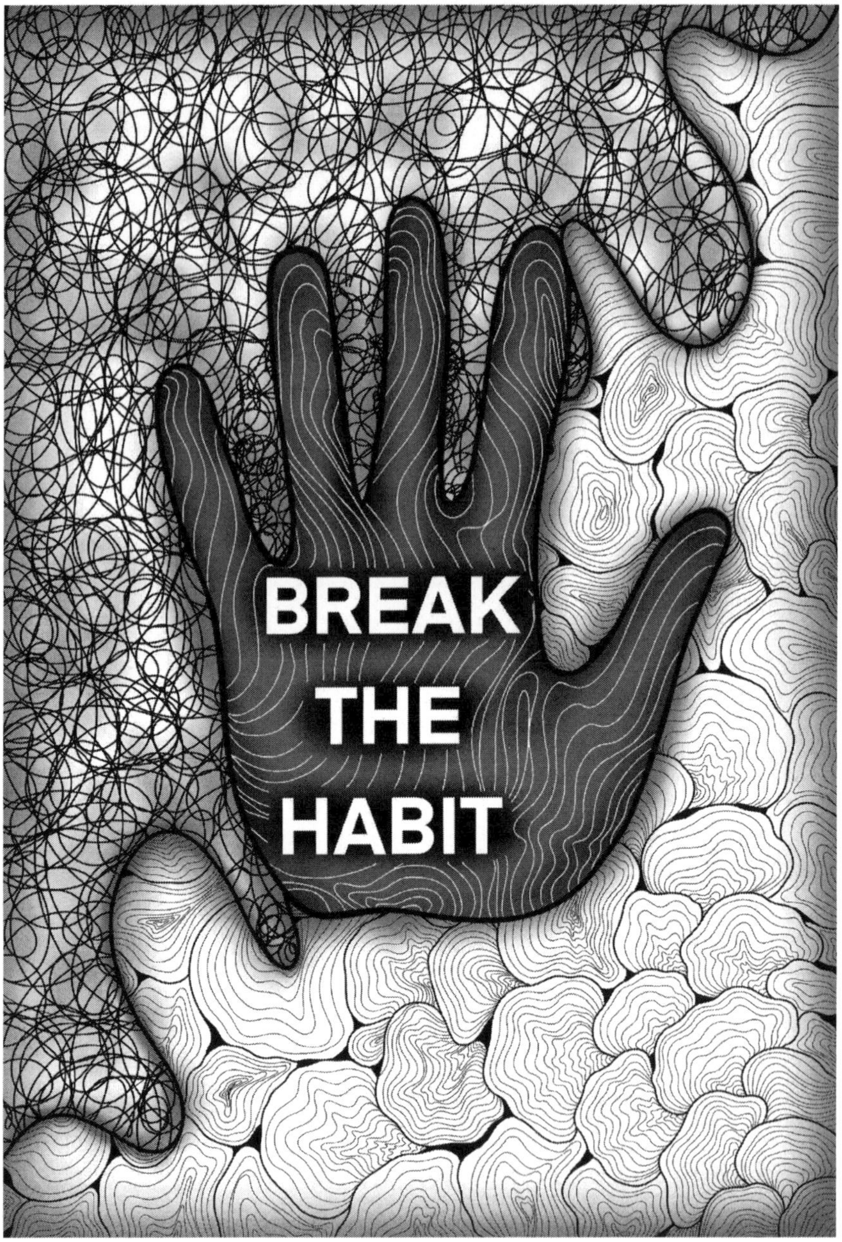
BREAK
THE
HABIT

Chapter 2

Breaking the Habits

of Overthinking

We can never obtain peace in the outer world until we make peace with ourselves. –Dalai Lama

The first time you had to speak in front of a crowd, you probably replayed every word afterward, wondering if you had said something wrong. Or maybe you've spent so much time stressing over a decision that you ended up making none at all. That's overthinking.

Your mind keeps analyzing thoughts, situations, or decisions to the point where it becomes exhausting. Sure, thinking critically about things is important, but when reflection turns into rumination, it can drain your energy, spike anxiety, and make even simple choices feel overwhelming.

How does this happen? When you're not actively focused on something, a part of your brain called the default mode network (DMN) kicks in. This system is responsible for self-reflection and daydreaming, but for overthinkers, it can go into overdrive, keeping you stuck in endless loops of "What if?" and "I should have…"

Additionally, there are neurotransmitters like serotonin and dopamine, which help regulate mood and focus. When they're out of balance, overthinking can feel even more intense, making it harder to shift your attention or find peace of mind.

Statistics indicate that at least 40 million Americans face anxiety disorders, which are most common among those aged 18 years and older (Anxiety and Depression Association of America, 2022). Anxiety can be a tough cycle to break. It's easy to convince yourself that if you just think about something long enough, you'll arrive at the perfect solution. But that's rarely how it works.

Common Triggers of Overthinking

Overthinking often stems from deeply ingrained emotional and psychological patterns. Understanding these triggers is the first step toward breaking the cycle. Below, we discuss the most common catalysts for overthinking:

Perfectionism: Perfectionism creates an unrelenting pressure to achieve flawlessness, often leading to excessive analysis and self-criticism. It is frequently rooted in early experiences, such as growing up in an environment where love or approval was conditional on achievement. It can also stem from societal or cultural expectations that equate success with perfection.

Perfectionists often replay past actions, obsessing over what they could have done better. They may also procrastinate, fearing that their efforts will not meet their own impossibly high standards. This can lead to burnout, anxiety, and a diminished sense of self-worth. Over time, it stifles creativity and risk-taking as the fear of failure becomes paralyzing.

Fear of Uncertainty: The human brain craves predictability and control. When faced with uncertainty, overthinkers often spiral into "what-if" scenarios, trying to anticipate every possible outcome. A fear of uncertainty can stem from past experiences where unpredictability led to negative outcomes. It may also be linked to anxiety disorders or a natural temperament that prefers structure and routine.

In such scenarios, overthinkers may obsessively plan for every contingency, second-guess decisions, or avoid making choices altogether. For example, someone might spend hours researching a simple purchase, fearing they will make the wrong decision.

Past Trauma: Trauma, whether from childhood or adulthood, can leave emotional scars that manifest as overthinking. Unresolved trauma often creates a loop of intrusive thoughts and memories, disrupting the brain's ability to process and store memories effectively. This can lead to flashbacks, nightmares, or persistent thoughts about the traumatic event.

Overthinkers might also hyper-focus on potential threats, as their brains remain stuck in a state of hypervigilance. Unaddressed trauma can lead to conditions such as PTSD, depression, or chronic anxiety. It also affects relationships, as the individual may struggle to trust others or feel safe in the world.

Stressful Life Events: Life transitions, whether positive or negative, can overwhelm the mind and trigger overthinking. These events often disrupt routines and create a sense of instability. Stressful events such as job loss, divorce, moving to a new city, or even positive changes like marriage or promotion can challenge our sense of identity and security. During such times, overthinkers may obsess over the details of the situation, worrying about the future or regretting past decisions. For example, someone who has lost their marriage might endlessly analyze their previous relationship or fear they will never find another partner.

Social and Environmental Factors: Beyond internal triggers, external factors can also play a significant role in fueling overthinking. For example, individuals on social media can be constantly exposed to curated versions of others' lives, leading to self-doubt and over-analysis of their achievements or appearance. Workplaces and academic settings that emphasize competition and performance can exacerbate perfectionism and fear of failure. Without a strong network of friends or family, individuals may internalize their struggles, leading to rumination and isolation.

Cognitive Habits and Personality Traits: Certain personality traits and cognitive patterns make individuals more prone to overthinking. Some people naturally have a more analytical mindset, which, while beneficial in moderation, can spiral into overthinking. Highly sensitive individuals (HSIs) are more attuned to their surroundings and emotions, making them more likely to dwell on their thoughts and feelings. Finally, a lack of confidence can lead to second-guessing and the need for constant validation from others.

Impact of Overthinking on Mental Health

Negative Cycle: When individuals dwell on their thoughts, they often spiral into a cycle of negativity. Someone might replay a past event in their mind, focusing on what they could have done differently, which can cause emotional distress.

Decision Paralysis: When faced with multiple choices, some people become overwhelmed by the details and potential outcomes. They may question each option intensely, weighing the pros and cons endlessly. For example, someone trying to choose a restaurant might stress over the menu, ambiance, reviews, and what their friends might think.

Sleep Disturbances: Many people find that racing thoughts keep them awake at night. They might lie in bed replaying the events of their day or worrying about tomorrow. For example, someone might think about a presentation they have to give or a conversation they had that did not go as planned. This state eventually leads to fatigue and further exacerbates overthinking.

Mental Clutter: Mental clutter is the overwhelming feeling of having too many thoughts competing for attention at once. Have you ever tried to listen to five different songs simultaneously? You can't focus on any of them, and it just leaves you feeling frazzled. Likewise, with mental clutter, it becomes difficult to concentrate, make decisions, or simply enjoy the moment.

So, where does all this clutter come from?

- **Technology Overload:** Notifications, emails, and social media create a never-ending stream of information that keeps our brains constantly "on."

- **Chaotic Environments:** A messy desk or a cluttered room can make your mind feel just as disorganized.

- **Life Stressors:** Work deadlines, family responsibilities, and even the pressure to keep up with everything can pile up, leaving us feeling overwhelmed.

If left unaddressed, it can lead to chronic stress, anxiety, and even burnout. According to Sander (2019), disorganized spaces can cause cognitive overload, making it difficult to focus and process information. Just as physical clutter requires organization, mental clutter necessitates structured interventions, like those described, to restore balance and productivity.

Mental clutter can create distance between us and the people we care about, making it harder to connect meaningfully. Dr. Ashley Solomon's work emphasizes that clearing mental space is essential for optimal functioning. She argues that mental clutter simulates chaos, leading to elevated stress levels and compromised decision-making capabilities (Solomon, 2023).

How to Start Clearing the Clutter

Here are some practical steps to help you declutter and find clarity:

1. **Set Boundaries with Technology:** Try turning off notifications or setting specific times to check your phone. Giving your brain a break from constant stimulation can make a huge difference.

2. **Tidy Up Your Space:** A clean, organized environment can help calm your mind. As the saying goes, "Outer order contributes to inner calm."

3. **Filter What You Consume:** Just as you set boundaries in relationships, you can set boundaries with your thoughts. Pay attention to what drains your mental energy. Maybe it's certain conversations, social media, or even watching too much negative news. Reducing exposure to these elements can significantly help in keeping your mind clear and focused.

4. **Practice Mindfulness:** Simple techniques like deep breathing or meditation can help anchor you in the present moment. When you notice your thoughts spiraling, take a few deep breaths and gently bring your focus back to the here and now.

Practical Ways to Worry Less

Here are simple, effective ways to loosen worry's grip and bring more peace into your life.

Thought Reframing: Our minds can be dramatic. A small mistake at work can turn into "I'm terrible at my job." A delayed response from a friend may become, "They must be mad at me." Thought reframing helps you catch these exaggerated thoughts and replace them with more balanced perspectives. Instead of thinking, "What if I fail?" try reframing it as, "Even if I struggle, I'll learn something valuable." Once you start noticing unhelpful thoughts, question them instead of automatically accepting them as truth.

Ask yourself:

- *Is there actual evidence for this thought, or is it just an assumption?*
- *Would I say this to a friend in the same situation?*
- *Is there a more balanced way to look at this?*

For example, instead of thinking, "I'm terrible at my job," try saying, "I made a mistake, but I can learn from it and do better next time." Small shifts like these can make a huge difference over time.

Give Worry a Time Slot: If worries keep hijacking your day, set aside a specific "worry time." Perhaps 15 minutes in the evening where you write down your concerns, acknowledge them, and then move on. This approach keeps worry from taking over your whole day while still providing a space for it to be heard.

Lean on Your Support System: Worry feels heavier when you carry it alone. Talking to a friend, family member, or therapist can help you gain new perspectives and feel less isolated. Sometimes, simply saying your worries out loud makes them feel smaller. If worry is taking a toll, seeking professional support, such as cognitive-behavioral therapy, can equip you with tools to break free from anxious thought patterns.

Practical Exercises to Stop Overthinking

It is possible to interrupt overthinking patterns and create mental space for calm and clarity. Below are practical, actionable exercises designed to help you achieve this:

1. **The 4-7-8 Breathing Technique:** This simple breathing exercise can instantly calm your mind:

- Inhale through your nose for 4 seconds.
- Hold your breath for 7 seconds.
- Exhale slowly through your mouth for 8 seconds.
- Try it a few times and notice how it helps reset your focus.

2. **Thought-Stopping:** When you catch yourself overthinking, try this:
    - Picture a big stop sign in your mind.
    - Say "STOP" out loud or in your head.
    - Immediately redirect your focus to something neutral or positive.
    - This isn't about ignoring problems—it's about stopping unnecessary mental loops before they spiral.

3. **Get Moving:** Physical activity is a great way to shake off overthinking. A quick walk, some stretching, or even a few yoga poses can help clear your mind. Moving your body shifts your focus away from anxious thoughts and back into the present.

4. **Journaling for Clarity:** Writing things down can be surprisingly powerful. Instead of letting thoughts swirl in your head, put them on paper. You might notice patterns or worries that repeat themselves. Once they're written down, they often feel less overwhelming.

5. **The 5-4-3-2-1 Grounding Technique:** This exercise helps bring your focus back to the present moment, interrupting spiraling thoughts. Here's how to do it:
    a. Identify five things you can see around you (e.g., a plant, a book, a window).
    b. Notice four things you can touch (e.g., your clothes, a table, your hair).
    c. Acknowledge three things you can hear (e.g., birds chirping, traffic, your breath).
    d. Recognize two things you can smell (e.g., coffee, fresh air).
    e. Identify one thing you can taste (e.g., toothpaste, a sip of water).

6. **Thought Labeling:** This exercise helps you detach from negative thoughts by observing them without judgment:

    a. When a negative thought arises, mentally label it. For example:

    - *This is a worry.*
    - *This is self-criticism.*
    - *This is rumination.*

    b. Imagine the thought of a cloud passing in the sky or a leaf floating down a stream. Let it drift away without holding onto it.

7. **Gratitude Practice:** Focusing on gratitude can counteract negativity and create a sense of calm.

    a. Each day, write down three things you're grateful for.

    b. Reflect on why these things matter to you.

8. **Body Scan Meditation:** This exercise helps you reconnect with your body and release tension.

    a. Sit or lie down in a comfortable position.

    b. Close your eyes and take a few deep breaths.

    c. Slowly scan your body from head to toe, noticing any areas of tension or discomfort.

    d. As you exhale, imagine releasing tension from each area.

9. **The "Not My Problem" List:** This exercise helps you let go of worries that are beyond your control.

    a. Write down all the things you're worried about.

    b. Divide them into two categories: (a) "Things I Can Control;" (b) "Things I Can't Control."

    c. Focus your energy on the "Things I Can Control" list and let go of the rest.

10. **Visualization of a Safe Space:** This exercise creates a mental refuge where you can retreat to feel calm.

a. Close your eyes and imagine a place where you feel safe and peaceful (e.g., a beach, a forest, or a cozy room).

   b. Visualize the details—sights, sounds, smells, and sensations.

   c. Spend a few minutes in this space, breathing deeply and relaxing.

11. **Progressive Muscle Relaxation:** This exercise helps release physical tension, which often accompanies negative thoughts.

    a. Sit or lie down in a comfortable position.

    b. Starting with your toes, tense the muscles for 5 seconds, then release.

    c. Move up your body, tensing and relaxing each muscle group (calves, thighs, abdomen, arms, etc.).

    d. Finish with your facial muscles and take a few deep breaths.

12. **Establish a Calming Routine**

Despite the unpredictability of life, we can still find a daily routine that allows us to remain consistent and nurture our mental clarity. A structured schedule helps reduce the chances of feeling overwhelmed by uncertainty.

Routines also provide a framework that encourages the development of healthy habits. For instance, they help us prioritize self-care and mindfulness.

You can make the most of your mornings by intentionally scheduling time for activities that calm your mind and nourish your soul. For example, starting with meditation or journaling can help clear your mind. Even a few minutes of focused breathing can ground you, preparing you for the day ahead.

You could also take a walk in your neighborhood, practice some gentle yoga, or simply stretch your arms overhead to engage your body, boosting your energy and mood. Finish it off with a healthy breakfast to fuel you for any challenges that come your way.

Limit your screen time during those early hours as well. Just think about how refreshing it is to enjoy your coffee without the buzz of notifications vying for your attention. Use that time to focus on the present moment, allowing yourself to cultivate gratitude for the day.

As your day unfolds, incorporate periodic mindfulness breaks to avoid getting lost in tasks and responsibilities. You can spare a few moments for intentional pauses, which create valuable space for mental relief. Perhaps take a quick stretch break to loosen up tight muscles accumulated from hours of sitting.

As evening approaches, establish practices that help you wind down. Journaling before bed can be a beautiful ritual for reflection and mental clarity.

Carry out some gentle stretching or relaxation techniques to signal to your body that it's time to slow down.

Prepare your mind for sleep, and once again, avoid screens to promote better rest.

***

Detaching from unhelpful thoughts may not happen completely, but you can begin taking small steps, such as practicing mindfulness, challenging negative thoughts, or setting mental boundaries, all of which can make a real difference. Your thoughts do not define you. You have the power to step back, take a breath, and create a little more peace in your mind. Let's explore how you can separate yourself from your thoughts in the next chapter.

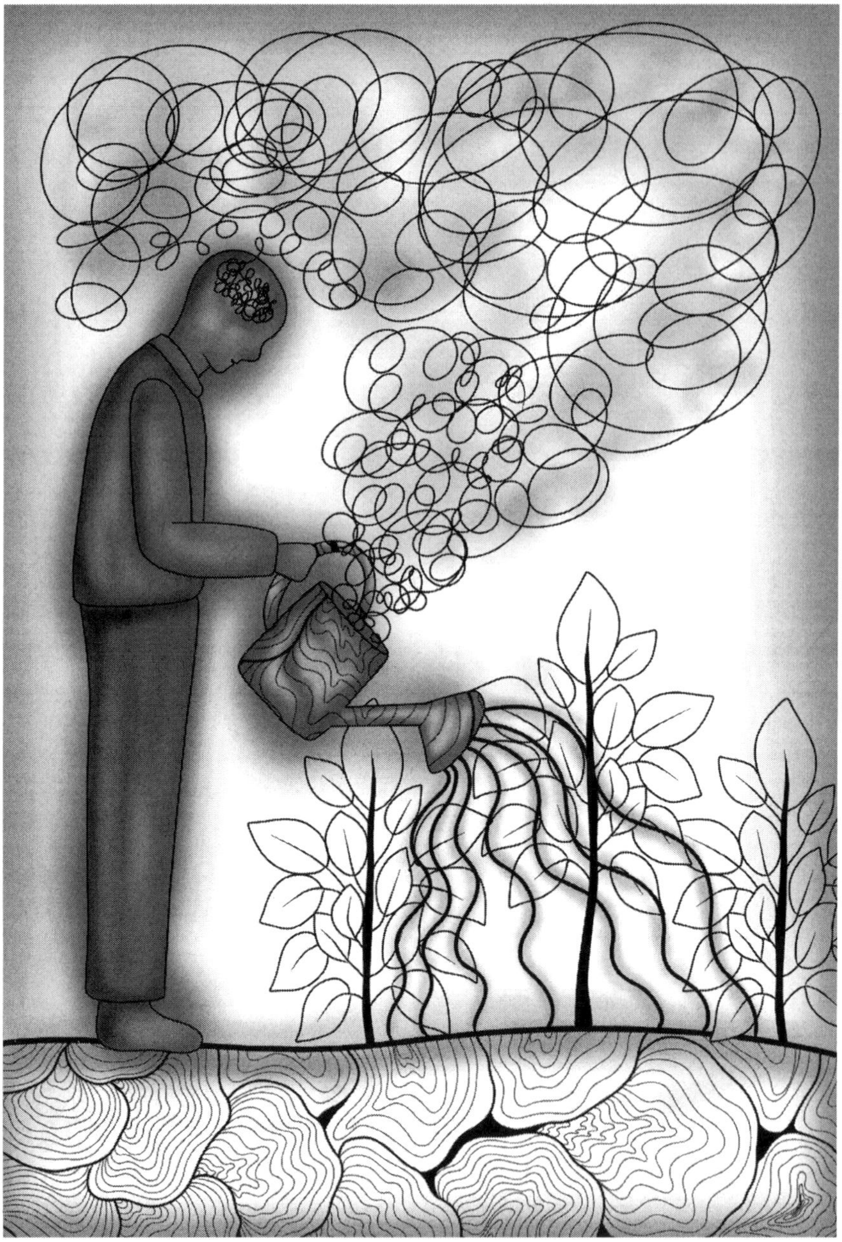

Chapter 3

Creating Space Between You and Your Thoughts

Peace is a daily, a weekly, a monthly process, gradually changing opinions, slowly eroding old barriers, quietly building new structures. –John F. Kennedy

How do you separate yourself from your thoughts, especially when your mind feels like a runaway train? While it may seem like your thoughts are nonstop, if you pay close attention, you'll find tiny gaps that you can take advantage of to create space between yourself and your thoughts.

This process, often referred to as cognitive defusion in psychology, involves stepping back from your thoughts and observing them without getting caught up in their emotional charge. This practice ensures that you can gain clarity, reduce stress, and respond to situations more intentionally, rather than reacting impulsively.

It all starts with awareness, which involves:

1. **Identifying Your Thoughts:** Awareness allows you to observe the flow of thoughts in your mind. For instance, when a thought arises—whether it is a worry, a fear, or a pleasant memory—take a moment to acknowledge it without reacting immediately.

2. **Understanding Thought Patterns:** Once you become aware of your thoughts, begin to notice patterns. Do certain thoughts arise more frequently? Are there specific triggers that lead to negative thinking? Understanding these patterns enables you to see how your thoughts influence your emotions and behaviors.

3. **Detaching from Thoughts:** The goal of awareness is not to eliminate thoughts but to create a space between you and them. By recognizing that thoughts are just thoughts rather than absolute truths, you start to detach from them. This perspective can help reduce their power over you, as you begin to understand that you are not defined by your thoughts.

4. **Practicing Mindfulness:** Mindfulness practices, such as meditation or focused breathing, can enhance your ability to cultivate awareness. These practices encourage you to observe your thoughts without judgment and gently guide your focus back to the present moment when distractions arise.

The Power of Labelling and Observing Thoughts

Although our minds are constantly buzzing with negative or positive thoughts, we can dominate them to avoid stress, anxiety, and emotional turmoil. We can learn to observe and label our thoughts to create a healthy distance from them, reducing their power over us. Here are some exercises to practice this.

1. **The "Thought Labeling" Journal**

Keep a journal in which you write down your thoughts and label them. When you begin to do this, you will start noticing common themes—certain fears, repeated worries, or internal criticisms that arise again and again.

Let your thoughts flow freely, and over time, you will begin to notice which ones serve you and which ones are just noise. Even five minutes of journaling each day can help you step outside your mental loops and make sense of what is going on inside. For example:

- o Thought: "I'll never be good enough." Label: "This is self-criticism."
- o Thought: "What if I mess up the presentation?" Label: "This is a worry."

2. **The "Mental Notepad" Exercise**

If writing feels too structured, try mind mapping. It's a creative way to visualize how your thoughts connect. Start with a central thought, such as "I am not enough," and draw branches to different areas where this belief affects you—work, relationships, and personal growth. Seeing these connections on paper makes it easier to challenge them. For example, if you realize that self-doubt in your career is rooted in a past experience, you can begin to separate that old story from your present reality. This visualization helps you practice observing and labeling your thoughts in real time.

3. Utilizing Mindful Labeling

Mindful labeling identifies thoughts for what they are instead of letting them dictate your emotions. Start by distinguishing between facts, opinions, and emotions:

- "I made a mistake" (fact) vs. "I'm a failure" (opinion)

- "I feel anxious" (emotion) vs. "Something terrible is going to happen" (prediction)

Recognizing this difference helps you evaluate your thoughts with greater clarity, reducing their emotional intensity.

Once you're comfortable labeling thoughts, take it a step further by reframing them. If your inner dialogue is filled with self-criticism, experiment with a more balanced perspective:

- Instead of "I always mess up," try "I'm learning and improving."

- Instead of "Nobody likes me," try "I'm working on building deeper connections."

Over time, this practice fosters self-compassion and resilience, making it easier to navigate challenges without being weighed down by self-doubt.

4. The "Thought Train" Visualization

- Picture your thoughts as passengers on a train. Label each passenger as they board (e.g., "This is anxiety," "This is planning").

This exercise reinforces the idea that thoughts are temporary and separate from you.

5. The "Balloon Release" Technique

- Imagine each thought as a balloon. Label the balloon (e.g., "This is self-doubt") and release it into the sky.

This visualization helps you practice letting go of thoughts after observing and labelling them.

6. The "Thoughts Are Just Stories" Exercise

- When a thought arises, remind yourself, "This is just a story my mind is telling me," and label it (e.g., "This is a fear story").

This exercise helps you see thoughts as narratives rather than facts.

7. **Reflection:** Close your eyes for just a moment and shift your focus—not on the thoughts themselves, but on the stillness in between. What does that feel like? What do you notice?

This practice is especially helpful when your mind is speeding up, convincing you that you need to do more, think harder, or figure everything out immediately. When we feel the urge to push forward, what we often need most is to slow down. Instead of getting caught in a cycle of overthinking, pausing in this way gives you the space to reset, shift your perspective, and approach challenges with greater clarity.

This won't erase problems or difficult emotions, and that's not the goal. Instead, it helps you step out of problem-solving mode and into a place of curiosity—where you're not trying to "fix" your thoughts but simply observing them with openness and awareness. In that space, you might just find the clarity you've been looking for.

8. **Identifying Triggers:** Once you recognize your patterns, figure out what sets them off. Maybe stressful meetings trigger negative self-talk, or social situations bring out your perfectionism. Once you identify your triggers, you can prepare for them rather than being caught off guard. Ask yourself:

    - When do I feel most anxious or overwhelmed?

    - Are there certain people, places, or situations that consistently affect my thoughts?

    - What physical or emotional states make me more vulnerable to overthinking?

Take a moment to picture a typical day. When does stress tend to creep in? Is it during your morning commute, after a conversation with a particular colleague, or at the end of a long meeting? These moments can help you start to uncover patterns regarding what triggers your stress and how it builds throughout the day, empowering you to respond intentionally instead of reacting automatically.

9. **Practice Mindful Awareness:** Simple exercises like breath awareness brings your attention back to the present when your mind feels scattered. You can turn to the simple, grounding rhythm of your breath. When you focus on each inhale and exhale, you create a pause, a moment of calm within the chaos.

To practice, find a quiet space, sit comfortably, and close your eyes. Let your breath flow naturally, following its rise and fall. If your mind starts to wander, gently bring it back to your breath—no judgment, just a quiet return. Over time, this simple practice cultivates a sense of stability, helping you to navigate difficult moments.

10. **Body Scan techniques:** These deepen the connection between your thoughts and physical sensations. Stress doesn't just stay in your mind—it settles in your body, tightening your shoulders, clenching your jaw, or weighing down your chest. A body scan brings awareness to these sensations, helping you release tension before it builds.

Lie down, close your eyes, and take a deep breath. Slowly direct your attention to different areas of your body, from the tips of your toes to the top of your head. Notice any tension or discomfort without trying to change it; simply acknowledge what is there. With practice, this technique enhances self-awareness, revealing how stress manifests physically and offering a path to relaxation.

11. **Daily Mindfulness Reminders:** Reinforcing these practices can keep you anchored in the present. Simple cues like a phone reminder, a sticky note on your desk, or a deep breath before checking emails can nudge you back to awareness. These small moments add up, training your mind to shift from autopilot to active presence.

As you practice these techniques, approach the process with curiosity and compassion. Explore your thoughts with an open mind. Ask yourself, "Why is this thought here?" or "What can I learn from this?"

Treat yourself with kindness, especially when you notice negative or self-critical thoughts. Remind yourself, "It's okay to have this thought; it doesn't define me."

The Long-Term Benefits

Over time, this practice can transform your relationship with your mind:

- **Reduced Stress:** You'll feel less overwhelmed by mental chatter.

- **Improved Emotional Regulation:** You'll be able to respond to situations with greater calm and clarity.

- **Greater Self-Awareness:** You'll gain insight into your thought patterns and emotional triggers.

- **Enhanced Presence:** You'll become more grounded in the present moment, rather than getting lost in the past or future.

Taking Time to Pause

Adding small pauses throughout the day can create a vital space between stress and reaction. Pausing interrupts the automatic cycle of stress and reaction. It gives you a moment to step back, breathe, and choose how you want to respond. The power of the pause is rooted in neuroscience and psychology:

- **The Amygdala and Prefrontal Cortex:** When you're stressed, your amygdala (the brain's fear center) activates, triggering a fight-or-flight response. Pausing engages the prefrontal cortex (the brain's rational center), allowing you to respond thoughtfully rather than react impulsively.

- **The Parasympathetic Nervous System:** Deep breathing during a pause activates the parasympathetic nervous system, which calms the body and reduces stress.

- **Neuroplasticity:** Regularly practicing pauses can rewire your brain, making it easier to respond calmly and intentionally over time.

How to Create a Pause

Pausing simply takes a moment to step back and breathe. Here's how to do it:

- **Notice the Trigger:** Become aware of the moment when stress or a strong emotion arises. This could be a tense conversation, a looming deadline, or a sudden change in plans. For instance, if you receive a critical email and feel your heart rate increase, that's a cue to respond differently.

- **Pause and Breathe:** Take a deep breath in through your nose, hold it for a moment, and exhale slowly through your mouth. Repeat this 2–3 times. Instead of immediately replying to the email, pause and take three deep breaths.

- **Observe Your Thoughts and Emotions:** Use this moment to observe what's happening internally. What thoughts are arising? What emotions are you feeling?

- Example: You notice the thought, "I'm being attacked," and the emotion of anger.

- **Choose Your Response:** With a calmer mind, decide how you want to respond. What action aligns with your values and goals? Instead of sending a defensive reply, choose to draft a calm and professional response.

Practical Strategies for Incorporating Pauses

Here are some simple ways to create pauses throughout your day:

1. **The "STOP" Technique**

Stop what you're doing.

Take a deep breath.

Observe your thoughts, feelings, and surroundings.

Proceed with intention.

2. **Set Pause Reminders**

Use alarms or notifications on your phone to remind yourself to pause at regular intervals (e.g., every hour).

Example: When the alarm goes off, take a moment to breathe and check in with yourself.

3. **Create Transition Pauses**

Pause between activities to reset and refocus. For example, take a few deep breaths before starting a new task or after finishing a meeting.

Example: After a busy work session, pause for a minute before moving on to the next task.

4. **Use Everyday Activities as Pause Triggers**

Turn routine activities into opportunities to pause. For example:

Pause before eating a meal to express gratitude.

Pause before entering your home to set an intention for how you want to be with your family.

Example: Before answering a phone call, take a deep breath and center yourself.

5. **Practice the "Three-Breath Pause"**

Whenever you feel stressed or overwhelmed, pause and take three deep breaths. Focus on the sensation of your breath entering and leaving your body.

Example: During a heated discussion, pause and take three breaths before responding.

6. Create a "Pause Ritual"

Develop a personal ritual that helps you pause and reset. This could be a short walk, a moment of stretching, or a mindfulness exercise.

Example: Every afternoon, step outside for a five-minute walk to clear your mind.

Overcoming Challenges to Pausing

It can be challenging to implement pausing in a busy life. Here are some tips to overcome common obstacles:

- **"I don't have time:"** Start with micro-pauses—even a few seconds of deep breathing can make a difference.

- **"I forget to pause:"** Use reminders or tie pauses to existing habits (e.g., pausing before checking your phone).

- **"It feels awkward:"** Remember that pausing is a skill that gets easier with practice. Start small and be patient with yourself.

***

We've explored practical strategies for creating space between ourselves and our thoughts. When we recognize common patterns, such as catastrophizing and overgeneralizing, we gain insight into how our minds shape our experiences. Techniques such as journaling and mind mapping help bring these patterns to light, providing us with the tools to reshape them.

Mindfulness practices—from breath awareness to body scans—offer a path to greater presence, helping us detach from negative thought cycles. Cognitive defusion and visualization techniques remind us that thoughts are fleeting, not fixed realities. Grounding exercises, thought labeling, and reframing encourage a shift in perspective, reinforcing a healthier and more compassionate relationship with our inner world. Let's discover how to do that in the next chapter.

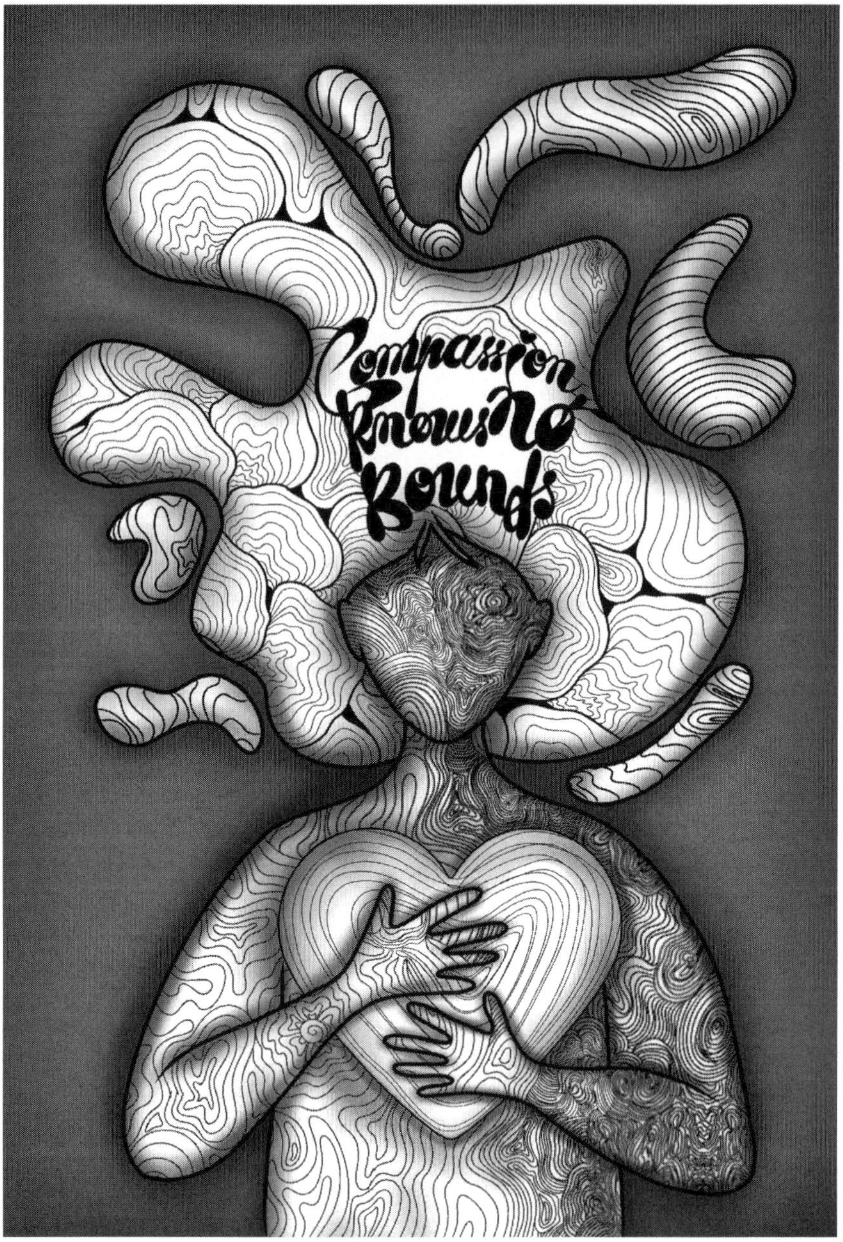
Compassion
Knows No
Bounds

Chapter 4

Cultivating Self-Compassion

You can observe a lot by just watching. (Implying the importance of mindfulness in achieving peace.) –Yogi Berra

When a friend or loved one stumbles, our first instinct is often to offer encouragement, understanding, and support rather than criticism. However, when we face our own missteps, do we extend the same compassion? Too often, we reserve kindness for others while holding ourselves to impossibly high standards. Learning to treat ourselves with the same grace we offer others can transform the way we navigate setbacks, foster growth, and ultimately empower us to thrive.

Self-compassion, as defined by Neff (2024), involves treating oneself with kindness, understanding, and support in times of suffering or perceived inadequacy. It encompasses three core components:

1. **Self-Kindness:** Being warm and understanding toward oneself when encountering pain or failure, rather than being harshly critical.

2. **Common Humanity:** Recognizing that suffering and personal shortcomings are part of the shared human experience, which makes it easier to feel connected to others rather than isolated.

3. **Mindfulness:** Maintaining a balanced awareness of one's emotions and allowing for a clear recognition of one's suffering without being overwhelmed by it.

Benefits of Self-Compassion

Although some people fear that self-kindness leads to complacency, research shows the opposite: When you create a space for self-acceptance, you actually feel safer taking risks, learning from failure, and pushing yourself forward. You gain the confidence to grow. Self-compassion impacts your mental, emotional, and even physical well-being. It helps you navigate life's challenges with greater resilience, kindness, and understanding.

Here are some key reasons why it matters:

- **Improves Mental Health:** Self-compassion helps you break free from the cycle of harsh self-judgment, which is often linked to anxiety, depression, and low self-esteem. This is because it activates the body's calming parasympathetic nervous system, reducing stress hormones like cortisol. You are able to approach challenges with calmness and perspective rather than being overwhelmed by fear or self-doubt. During difficult moments, you can build emotional strength and recover more quickly from setbacks.

- **Enhances Self-Worth:** It fosters a sense of intrinsic self-worth that isn't dependent on external achievements or validation. It reminds you that you are worthy of care and respect simply because you exist.

- **Encourages Healthy Relationships:** When you are compassionate toward yourself, you are better equipped to extend compassion to others. This creates healthier, more empathetic, and supportive relationships. It also helps you set boundaries and avoid people-pleasing behaviors, as you prioritize your own well-being. You are more likely to focus on your own needs and engage in self-care practices that nourish your mind, body, and spirit.

- **Promotes Personal Growth:** Self-compassion creates a safe space for self-reflection and learning. When you are not afraid of failure or judgment, you are more likely to take risks, try new things, and grow from your experiences. You view mistakes as opportunities for growth.

- **Supports Physical Health:** Research shows that self-compassion is linked to healthier lifestyle choices, such as better sleep, regular exercise, and balanced eating. It also reduces inflammation and supports the immune system, contributing to overall physical well-being.

- **Fosters Mindfulness:** Self-compassion encourages you to stay present with your emotions and experiences without judgment. You are able to respond to life's challenges with clarity and intention rather than reacting impulsively.

- **Helps You Feel Less Isolated:** Self-compassion reminds you that everyone struggles and makes mistakes. This sense of common humanity can alleviate feelings of loneliness and isolation.

- **Leads to Greater Happiness:** You are in a better position to cultivate a more positive and accepting relationship with yourself when you practice self-kindness, which contributes to greater overall happiness and life satisfaction.

Simple Ways to Nurture Self-Kindness

With small, intentional changes, you can cultivate self-kindness. Here are a few ways to start:

- **Reframe Your Inner Dialogue:** Pay attention to how you speak to yourself. If your self-talk is filled with phrases like "I'm such a failure" or "I'll never get this right," pause and reframe it. Try saying, "I'm learning and growing" or "I'm doing my best, and that's enough."

- **Use Daily Affirmations:** Affirmations might feel awkward at first, but they can shift the way you see yourself over time. Start your morning with a simple phrase like, *I am worthy of kindness,* or *I give myself permission to be imperfect.* Set reminders on your phone or write them on sticky notes where you can see them throughout the day.

- **Talk to Yourself Like a Friend:** When you make a mistake, ask yourself, *What would I say to a loved one in this situation?* Then apply that same kindness to yourself.

- **Practice Mindfulness:** Stay present with your thoughts and feelings without judgment. Mindfulness helps you acknowledge struggles without becoming overwhelmed by them.

- **Embrace Imperfection:** Accept that making mistakes is part of being human. Perfection isn't the goal—growth is.

- **Set Healthy Boundaries:** Protect your mental and emotional well-being by saying no when necessary, resting when needed, and prioritizing self-care.

- **Celebrate Small Wins:** Recognize and appreciate your efforts, no matter how minor. Progress, not perfection, is what matters.

- **Engage in Self-Care:** Prioritize activities that nourish you, whether it's resting, exercising, journaling, or spending time in nature.

- **Surround Yourself with Supportive People:** Spend time with those who uplift and encourage you rather than those who drain or criticize.

- **Forgive Yourself:** Let go of past mistakes and acknowledge that growth comes from experience, not from self-punishment.

Silencing Your Inner Critic

Quieting the inner critic and reframing negative self-talk are essential for cultivating self-compassion and building a healthier relationship with yourself. Here are some practical strategies to help you silence that critical voice and replace it with more supportive and constructive thoughts:

- **Awareness and Identification:** Pay attention to when your inner critic shows up. What triggers it? What does it say? Then give your inner critic a name (e.g., "The Judge" or "The Perfectionist"). This helps you separate it from your true self and see it as just one part of you, not the whole.

- **Use Self-Compassion Phrases:** When you notice self-criticism, pause and say kind, supportive things to yourself, such as, "This is hard, but I'm doing my best," or "I'm allowed to make mistakes; it's part of being human." You can also write a letter to yourself as if you were a compassionate friend, offering understanding and encouragement.

- **Adopt a Growth Mindset:** Instead of seeing mistakes as failures, view them as opportunities to learn and grow. Ask yourself, "What can I take away from this experience?"

- **Use Mindfulness Techniques:** Use grounding techniques, like deep breathing or focusing on your senses, to bring yourself back to the present moment when self-criticism arises.

- **Create a Supportive Inner Dialogue:** Create a positive mantra or affirmation to counter negative self-talk. For example, you can say, "I am enough" or "I am worthy of love and respect." Imagine a kind, supportive person (real or imagined) speaking to you with compassion and encouragement.

- **Limit Comparisons:** Social media often fuels comparison and self-criticism. Limit your time on these platforms or curate your feed to include positive, uplifting content. Remind yourself that everyone's path is different, and your worth isn't determined by how you measure up to others.

- **Seek External Support:** Share your struggles with someone you trust. Sometimes, an outside perspective can help you see yourself more clearly and compassionately. Connecting with others who are working on similar challenges can also provide encouragement and accountability.

- **Use Humor:** Sometimes, humor can disarm the inner critic. Imagine your inner critic as a cartoon character with a silly voice, or laugh at the absurdity of its harsh statements.

- **Affirm Your Strengths:** Write down your achievements, big and small, to remind yourself of your capabilities. Reflect on your positive qualities and how they have helped you in the past.

Stories of Self-Kindness in Action

Self-Doubt to Self-Compassion: Healing Through Gratitude

As told by Terry

As my 32nd birthday approached, I found myself spiraling into self-doubt. Beyond the flood of cheerful birthday messages, a deeper, quieter voice whispered unsettling questions: *What have I really accomplished?*

I watched as my friends celebrated milestones—marriages, children, promotions—while I stood on the sidelines, feeling like a failure. I should have made more money by now. I should have broken through in my business. I should have… The list was endless, and with each unfulfilled expectation, the weight of regret grew heavier.

Then came the cruelest realization: Maybe I was the reason for my own failures. The mistakes I had made—big, costly mistakes—paraded through my mind, each one accusing me. The weight of it all dragged me into a temporary state of depression, where I felt like I didn't belong anywhere.

But then, in the midst of that storm of self-recrimination, a memory surfaced. I was seven years old when one of my neighbors, an eight-year-old girl, was struck by a car. For the next decade, she lived in a wheelchair, battling health complications until she eventually passed away. Yet what I remembered most vividly wasn't her suffering but her joy. Even during those difficult years, she laughed, played, and embraced life with a resilience that defied her circumstances. I remember wheeling her around the neighborhood, her smile lighting up even the gloomiest days. She didn't live long, but she lived without regret.

As this memory settled over me, a different voice arose within—softer, quieter, yet steady and insistent. It was the voice of self-compassion.

Yes, I may not be where I expected to be, but there is so much to be grateful for: my family, my friends, my mentors… the journey itself. Slowly, I chose to amplify this quiet voice and give it space to grow. Unlike the self-critical voice, self-compassion has been patient with me.

Self-compassion gave me the freedom to move beyond my mistakes without getting stuck in them. It taught me that I didn't have to dwell on my failures or let them define me. Whenever I turned to it, it welcomed me with open arms, offering a sense of peace and understanding I hadn't allowed myself to feel before.

You see, for a long time, I had ignored it. I thought that if I embraced it, I'd be making excuses for my shortcomings. If I showed myself kindness, wouldn't that mean I was justifying my mistakes? Wouldn't that make me weak or complacent? These fears kept me trapped in a cycle of self-criticism and shame, where I believed that being hard on myself was the only way to grow.

However, gradually, I came to understand that self-compassion is not about denial; it's a profound path to self-awareness. That doesn't mean I ignore my flaws or pretend everything is perfect. I've learned to acknowledge my shortcomings with honesty while holding space for growth and transformation. I'm no longer defined by my imperfections.

It has now been more than three years since I embraced this practice. I still face setbacks and challenges—life doesn't stop being difficult just because you're kinder to yourself. These struggles have shaped me in ways I never expected, teaching me resilience I didn't know I had. They have also deepened my empathy and helped me uplift those who are susceptible to shame.

One of the greatest joys in my life now is walking alongside individuals battling addiction. There is something incredibly powerful about witnessing their journey— seeing their faces light up when they take those small, courageous steps toward recovery. It's in those moments that I'm reminded of the transformative power of compassion, both for ourselves and for others, and for that, I'm grateful.

How a Mindfulness Class Transformed My Life

As told by Christine

"One of the most transformative experiences of my life occurred during a mindfulness class I took in high school. At the time, I didn't realize how much it would shape me, but looking back, it was the beginning of a journey toward self-compassion that has profoundly impacted my adult life.

Back then, I was struggling significantly. My freshman and junior years were particularly rough. Anxiety and depression weighed heavily on me, and I didn't have the tools to cope. I often skipped school, stayed home, and allowed the stress to consume me to the point where it made me physically ill. I felt like I was drowning, and I didn't know how to come up for air.

That mindfulness class was my lifeline. It taught me something I hadn't considered before: the power of self-compassion. I learned to show myself loving-kindness and to accept all parts of myself—even the aspects that felt messy, such as when I was stressed or angry. I began to understand that I didn't have to fixate on my stress or mistakes. Instead, I could acknowledge them with compassion and remind myself, "This isn't everything in my life right now."

If I had known this earlier, I believe my high school experience would have been very different. Instead of allowing anxiety and depression to control me, I could have approached my struggles with more understanding and grace. I might have gained more from school—and life—if I had been kinder to myself.

Growing up, I had always been influenced by what I now refer to as the "conditioned mind." It was that voice in my head telling me, "You should dress like this," or "They will think this about you because of what you said." It was the voice of societal expectations, and I didn't even realize it wasn't my own. The mindfulness class opened my eyes to this. I learned that the first thought that pops into your head isn't always the truth—it's often just what you've been taught to think. But you don't have to believe it. You can pause, reflect, and choose a kinder, more constructive perspective.

Today, as an adult, self-compassion is something I actively practice. It's not always easy, but it has become a guiding principle in my life. When I make a mistake, I no longer immediately think, "I'm stupid." Instead, I remind myself, "I messed up, but what can I learn from this?" This shift in mindset has helped me navigate challenges with resilience and grace. It has allowed me to grow in ways I never thought possible. I've learned to extend the same kindness and understanding to others that I now offer myself.

My Journey to Self-Acceptance and True Well-Being

As told by Kathy

There was a time when I didn't have a good relationship with my body. In college, I pushed myself too hard—exercising excessively, obsessing over food, and chasing an impossible standard. People even made comments about how much I worked out, but I ignored them. Deep down, I thought that if I just controlled my body enough, I'd finally feel good enough.

For so long, I believed that my worth was tied to how I looked. Society made it easy to think that way; everywhere I turned, I was bombarded with messages that equated thinness with health, happiness, and success. Even the medical field reinforced this idea. Diet culture thrived on the promise that I just needed to lose a little more and do a little better.

But at some point, I realized that I was exhausted—physically, mentally, and emotionally. I had spent years being so hard on myself. The constant self-criticism wasn't making me healthier; it was making me miserable. So, I made a decision: I was going to practice self-kindness.

At first, it felt unnatural. I had spent so long tearing myself down that being kind to myself felt indulgent, almost wrong. But I started small. Instead of punishing workouts, I moved my body in ways that felt good—sometimes that meant yoga, a walk, or even just resting. I stopped labeling foods as good or bad and allowed myself to eat without guilt. And when negative thoughts crept in, I challenged them. I asked myself, *would I speak to a friend this way?* If the answer was no, then I didn't deserve to speak to myself that way either.

I also began to redefine what health meant to me. I realized that true health isn't about extremes but about balance. It's about knowing that a strong, fit body can come in different shapes and sizes. Most importantly, it's about peace.

This shift wasn't instant, and it wasn't easy. However, over time, as I showed myself more compassion, I noticed something incredible: I felt lighter. Not because I lost weight, but because I let go of the relentless pressure to be more. I was already enough.

Now, as a mother, I think about what I want to pass down to my daughter. I don't want her to grow up believing that her happiness depends on the number on a scale or the size of her jeans. I want her to know that she is enough exactly as she is.

And the only way to teach her that is by living it myself: by choosing self-kindness, by treating my body with respect, and by reminding myself every single day that I am already worthy.

***

Silencing your inner critic is a process of learning to meet yourself with patience and kindness. As you integrate these practices into your life, remember that progress is what matters. Over time, you will notice that your perspective on success, failure, and self-worth begins to shift. You will replace judgment with understanding and fear with self-trust. Ultimately, you will build a life in which your inner voice is not your harshest critic but your biggest supporter.

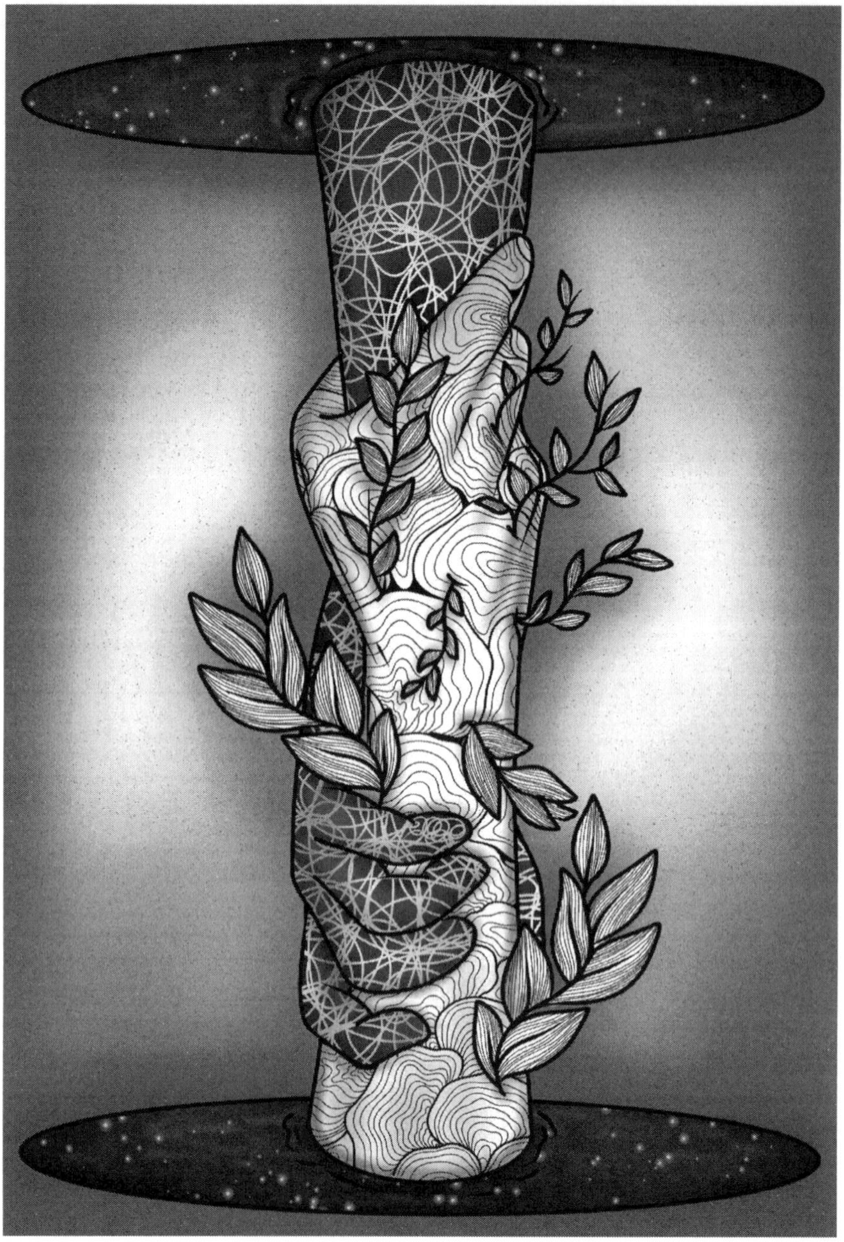

Chapter 5

Connecting to the Present Moment

Peace cannot be kept by force; it can only be achieved by understanding. –
Albert Einstein

Life sometimes moves too fast. When caught between endless to-do lists, notifications, and worries about the past or future, it's easy to feel as if you're being pulled in a hundred directions at once. But what if you could pause, connect with the present, and experience a sense of calm, clarity, and joy daily?

Individuals who experience this connection can feel a variety of things. They may notice when their shoulders feel as though they are carrying the weight of the world. Others may take a deep breath and instantly feel a little calmer. That's a sign that their thoughts, emotions, and physical sensations are constantly influencing one another.

That's the power of mindfulness. You are able to pay attention to what's happening at the moment. For instance, it could be the way your breath moves through your body, the tension in your jaw after a tough day, or the warmth that spreads when you feel happy. As a result, you give yourself the space to respond rather than react. The more you practice, the easier it becomes to find little moments of calm, even amid a hectic day.

How Mindfulness Helps You Tune Into the Present

When you focus on bodily sensations, you anchor yourself in the "here and now," which can help you break free from rumination about the past or worries about the future.

Here's how it works:

Body Awareness

Pay attention to your body. Say you're seated at your desk, and suddenly, you feel your shoulders creeping up toward your ears. The moment you notice, pause, roll them back, and take a deep breath. That simple shift can reset your whole mood. If you've ever tried yoga, tai chi, or even just stretching after waking up, you know how movement can bring focus and calm.

Picture yourself in a yoga class, slowly moving from one pose to another, feeling the stretch, the balance, and the strength in your muscles. Or imagine practicing tai chi, flowing through each movement with intention. These moments teach us how to be here now, instead of being lost in our thoughts.

You can also try this: Let's say you love walking through a lush park. Instead of rushing through, distracted by thoughts, pause. Notice the way the sunlight filters through the leaves, the gentle rustling of branches in the breeze, and the scent of damp earth after a fresh rain. These details pull you into the moment, offering an anchor that quiets the constant hum of the mind.

Body Scanning

Body scanning, a simple yet powerful practice, can help you tune into physical sensations. Try this:

1. Find a quiet place to sit or lie down.
2. Close your eyes and bring your attention to the top of your head.
3. Slowly scan down your body, noticing any areas of tension, warmth, or relaxation.
4. Acknowledge these sensations without judgment—just observe.

To truly integrate body awareness into your life, maintain consistency. Try setting aside a few moments each morning to scan your body and center yourself before the day begins. Short awareness breaks throughout the day—perhaps during lunch or before bed—can help you recalibrate and release tension before it builds up.

If you're new to this practice, start small. Take five minutes in the morning to stretch while paying attention to your breath. Stand up and move throughout the day, even if it's just rolling your shoulders or walking with awareness. Over time, these small acts of mindfulness add up. The more you engage with your body's sensations, the more naturally mindfulness becomes woven into your daily life.

Mindful Breathing

We breathe every second, yet we rarely think about it. But what if I told you that your breath could be your greatest tool for staying grounded, even in life's most chaotic moments? When stress, distractions, or emotions start knocking, returning to your breath provides a reliable point of stability. How can we then harness it beyond regular breathing?

Most of us breathe in a shallow, unconscious way—quick, light breaths from the chest. However, when we take slow, deep breaths from the belly, we tap into a powerful calming mechanism in the body. This is called diaphragmatic breathing (or belly breathing), and it's a simple yet effective way to relax your nervous system and bring yourself back to the present moment. Try this:

1. Find a quiet spot where you can sit or lie down comfortably.

2. Place one hand on your chest and the other on your belly.

3. Inhale deeply through your nose, feeling your belly rise (while keeping your chest still).

4. Exhale slowly through your mouth, feeling your belly fall.

5. Repeat for a few minutes, noticing how each breath brings a little more calm.

The more you do it, the more instinctive it becomes—so when stress sneaks up on you, you naturally turn to your breath instead of reacting impulsively. Here's a simple way to build a habit:

- Start with just 3–5 minutes a day.

- Set reminders—maybe a gentle alarm on your phone or a sticky note on your desk.

- Tie it to something you already do, like taking a few deep breaths before meals or as soon as you wake up.

Alternatively, you can try out another breathing method by following these steps:

Step 1: Find a Comfortable Position

- Sit comfortably with your back straight, shoulders relaxed, and hands resting on your lap.
- If you prefer, you can lie down or stand. The key is to feel at ease and alert.

Step 2: Center Yourself in the Present Moment

- Gently close your eyes or soften your gaze.
- Take a deep breath in, filling your lungs, and slowly exhale.
- Notice the sensation of the air flowing in and out.

Step 3: Begin Conscious Breathing

- Inhale deeply through your nose for a count of four (1…2…3…4).
- Hold your breath for a count of two (1…2).
- Exhale slowly through your mouth for a count of six (1…2…3…4…5…6).
- Pause briefly before inhaling again.
- Repeat this cycle for 5 to 10 minutes.

As you breathe, imagine each inhale as an embrace of life, and each exhale as a release of separation.

Step 4: Cultivating the Sense of Oneness

As you breathe mindfully, visualize:

- The air entering your lungs is the same air breathed by all living beings.
- Your breath merges with the rhythm of the wind, the trees, and the ocean waves.

- Every inhale draws in peace and unity, and every exhale dissolves barriers and separation.

Silently affirm:

- "With each breath, I am connected to all of life."

- "I inhale unity; I exhale division."

- "I am one with the universe, and the universe is one with me."

Step 5: Closing the Practice

- Slowly bring your awareness back to your surroundings.

- Wiggle your fingers and toes, gently opening your eyes.

- Take a moment to express gratitude for this moment of connection.

You can always practice these exercises from anywhere at any time, whether you're stuck in traffic, feeling overwhelmed at work, or lying awake at night.

As you practice these exercises, you'll notice that:

Your breath can change with your emotions. When you're anxious, it becomes shallow and rapid. When you're relaxed, it's slow and deep. Tuning into these patterns can provide you with incredible insight into your emotional state.

On the flip side, when you feel calm and at ease, your breath moves effortlessly. Recognizing these connections helps reinforce the idea that you have more control over your inner world than you might think.

Mindfulness as a Spiritual and Scientific Force

Mindfulness is also deeply rooted in the spiritual and scientific aspects of life. Many traditions incorporate mindfulness as a key component for growth and self-discovery. For instance, in Buddhism, mindfulness is an essential part of meditation. Practitioners sit quietly, focusing on their breath and observing their thoughts without judgment. This practice helps them gain insights into their minds and feelings.

From a scientific perspective, mindfulness has been extensively studied for its benefits to mental health and overall well-being. Research shows that practicing mindfulness can reduce stress, anxiety, and depression because it teaches the brain to respond to stress more effectively. Below, I will explain how the practice influences both aspects.

Oneness in Spiritual Traditions

Throughout history, spiritual traditions across cultures have recognized and honored the concept of oneness. For example:

- Buddhism teaches the concept of interbeing, where all things arise in dependence upon one another.

- Hinduism speaks of Advaita (non-duality), which is the realization that the self (Atman) is one with the ultimate reality (Brahman).

- Christianity emphasizes unity with God through love and service, as expressed in teachings such as, "The Kingdom of God is within you."

- Sufism (Islamic mysticism) describes divine love as the process of dissolving the self into the Beloved, where no separation remains.

These traditions, despite their differences, point to the same truth: that we are not separate but deeply interconnected with all existence.

Science and the Interconnected Universe

Modern science echoes ancient wisdom in understanding oneness:

- Quantum physics suggests that particles, once connected, remain entangled, regardless of the distance.

- Neuroscience reveals that human emotions and consciousness are deeply affected by collective experiences.

- Ecology demonstrates that all life forms exist in a delicate balance, interdependent and inseparable.

From these scientific insights, we can see that oneness is a reality that we can experience directly through mindful awareness.

The Breath as a Bridge to Oneness

Every living being, from the tiniest insect to the tallest tree, is part of this constant exchange, taking in oxygen and releasing carbon dioxide. It's a quiet, invisible rhythm that connects us to all of life.

But how often do we notice it?

When we shift our focus from just our breath to the bigger picture—the shared breath of the world—we start to feel something deeper. It's a doorway to something much larger. Here's what I mean.

From the moment we take our first inhale as newborns to the moment we exhale for the last time; our breath is with us. It's a constant reminder that we are alive, here, and connected.

Ancient traditions have always understood this. In Hinduism, the word *prana* refers to breath as the very life force that keeps us going. In Buddhism, mindful breathing (*anapanasati*) is a practice that helps dissolve the illusion of separateness. Even in Christianity, the Holy Spirit—*pneuma* in Greek, which means "breath" or "wind"—is seen as the divine presence that sustains all life.

Across cultures and beliefs, the message is the same: Breath is more than air; it's a connection to something greater than ourselves.

Think about it: When you breathe in, where does your breath stop and the world's breath begin? The air you inhale has passed through trees, oceans, and the lungs of every living creature before you. Every exhale you release becomes part of that same cycle.

A simple way to feel this connection is to imagine the entire universe breathing with you. As you inhale, picture life itself expanding; as you exhale, feel your breath merging back into the collective. The boundaries of "me" and "you" start to fade, and in their place, there is just presence—just being.

Breathing in Awareness, Breathing Out Compassion

Once we realize how connected we are, something shifts in the way we see others. Suddenly, compassion becomes a natural response.

- When we see someone struggling, we can breathe in, acknowledging their pain, and breathe out, sending kindness.

- When we're in conflict, a deep breath can remind us that the person in front of us is not separate from us; they, too, are part of this same great whole.

- When we feel lonely, simply focusing on our breath reminds us that we are never truly alone.

This is the foundation of practices like Loving-Kindness Meditation (*Metta*), through which we send goodwill to others using our breath and awareness.

The Breath Reflects the Mind

Our breath is also a mirror; it shows us what is happening inside. When we are anxious, it is shallow and quick. When we are calm, it is deep and steady. By simply observing our breath without trying to change it, we learn to witness our emotions in the same way: with curiosity instead of judgment.

Instead of labeling experiences as "good" or "bad," we start to see them like the breath—just passing through. Joy, sadness, stress, and love are all part of the same cycle, just like inhales and exhales. There is no need to cling to one or resist another; everything is part of the greater whole.

By returning to the breath repeatedly, we cultivate a sense of balance. We learn to meet life's ups and downs with presence rather than resistance. In that space of stillness, we find something incredible: a deep sense of connection, where nothing is separate, and everything simply is.

Breathing With Nature: The Earth as Our Reflection

Practicing mindfulness in nature is a profound way to experience oneness through breath. The natural world breathes just as we do:

- Trees inhale carbon dioxide and exhale oxygen, providing the very air we need to live.

- Rivers flow effortlessly, mirroring the way breath moves through us without force.

- The ocean's waves rise and fall in rhythm, much like our own inhalations and exhalations.

Sitting quietly in a natural setting and aligning your breath with the rhythm of nature deepens the experience of connection. You begin to realize that there is no fundamental separation between you and the world around you; you are a part of nature, just as the trees, rivers, and mountains are.

Experiencing Present Gratitude

Every day brings its fair share of frustrations. There is always something that doesn't go as planned, something to grumble about. But have you ever noticed that, just as surely, every day also offers something to be grateful for? The problem is that we often get so caught up in the busyness of life that we overlook the little moments of gratitude hidden in the chaos.

Gratitude shifts our perspective. It draws us into the present moment and helps us recognize the beauty woven into everyday life. It could be the warmth of the morning sun on your skin, the aroma of freshly brewed coffee, or the laughter of a loved one. When we take the time to acknowledge these small joys, we redirect our attention away from stress and toward the abundance that already exists around us.

You can start practicing gratitude through simple acts like journaling. Set aside a few moments each day to write down three things you are grateful for. That way, you cultivate a habit of reflection that extends beyond mere list-making. Over time, you begin to notice recurring themes—patterns of joy, moments of kindness, and sources of fulfillment that may have previously gone unnoticed. However, it can also be expressed through:

- **Verbal appreciation:** Telling someone how much they mean to you.

- **Creative expression:** Capturing gratitude through art, music, or photography.

- **Mindful reflection:** Taking a quiet moment to mentally recount what you're thankful for before bed.

Studies show that individuals who regularly practice gratitude report higher levels of happiness, better emotional regulation, and stronger social connections.

For instance, according to Penn State Pro Wellness (2022), more than 90% of American teenagers and adults reported feeling "extremely happy" or "somewhat happy" when they expressed gratitude. Additionally, maintaining a regular gratitude journal is linked to a 5% to 15% increase in optimism and a 25% improvement in sleep quality.

When we focus on what we appreciate, we gradually reframe our mindset. Instead of viewing challenges as obstacles, we begin to see them as opportunities for growth. Rather than being weighed down by negativity, we become more resilient in the face of adversity.

Gratitude acts as a buffer against stress and uncertainty, providing a stable foundation even in difficult times. When we consistently choose to see the good, we develop a sense of contentment that is less dependent on external circumstances and more rooted in inner peace.

At first, finding things to be grateful for might feel challenging—especially in moments of hardship. But, like any habit, gratitude strengthens with practice. Over time, even the smallest blessings become more apparent. With daily care, those seeds take root, growing into a mindset that naturally gravitates toward appreciation.

Other Practices to Connect to the Present Moment Through the Body

Here are some mindfulness techniques to help you tune into your bodily sensations and strengthen the mind-body connection:

Grounding Techniques

- **5-4-3-2-1 Exercise:** Identify five things you can see, four things you can touch, three things you can hear, two things you can smell, and one thing you can taste. This helps you connect with your senses and the present moment.

- **Feet on the Ground:** Notice the sensation of your feet touching the floor. This simple act can help you feel more grounded and present.

Noticing Daily Sensations: Throughout the day, pause to check in with your body. For example, notice the feeling of water on your hands while washing dishes, feel the texture of your clothes against your skin, or pay attention to the taste and texture of your food as you eat.

Posture and Presence: Believe it or not, the way you carry yourself can influence how present you feel. An open, relaxed posture—shoulders down, chest open—not only looks confident but also helps you feel more grounded.

Try this: Every so often, check in with your posture. Are you hunched over your phone? Tensed up at your desk? Take a moment to adjust. A small shift in the way you sit or stand can help bring your awareness back to the present.

Alexander Technique: Alternatively, you can try the Alexander Technique. Developed by F.M. Alexander in the late 19th century, this method teaches individuals to recognize and change habitual patterns of movement and posture that may cause tension, pain, or inefficiency. It emphasizes the connection between the mind and body, encouraging individuals to move with greater ease, balance, and coordination.

The technique teaches you to pay attention to how you use your body in everyday activities, such as sitting, standing, walking, or even speaking. As you become more aware of these habits, you can learn to release unnecessary tension and move more naturally and efficiently.

Guided Practice Through Videos: Mindful videos make it easier for beginners to engage in mindfulness. These instructions can help you stay focused and relaxed, reducing distractions. The combination of calming visuals and soothing sounds or narrations creates a serene atmosphere that promotes relaxation and awareness. The videos are also structured to teach specific mindfulness techniques, providing clarity and direction in your practice. Additionally, they are helpful for establishing a routine around your practice. This consistency can lead to improved mental clarity and emotional well-being over time.

Exercise: The Five Senses Grounding Technique

This exercise uses your five senses to anchor you in the present moment. It's particularly helpful when you're feeling stressed, anxious, or distracted.

Steps to Practice

1. **Find a Comfortable Position:** Sit or stand in a comfortable position.

2. **Take a Deep Breath:** Begin by taking a few deep breaths. Inhale slowly through your nose, hold for a moment, and exhale through your mouth. This helps calm your mind and prepare you for the exercise.

3. **Engage Your Five Senses:** What do you see, feel, hear, smell, and taste? For each sense, take a moment to notice and describe what you're experiencing. Try to focus fully on each sensation without judgment. Look around and notice five things you can see. They can be big or small, near or far.

Example: "I see the blue sky, a tree outside the window, my coffee mug, a pen on my desk, and a picture on the wall."

Notice four things you can feel. Pay attention to textures, temperatures, or sensations.

Example: "I feel the soft fabric of my shirt, the coolness of the air, the smooth surface of my desk, and the pressure of my feet on the floor."

Listen carefully and identify three sounds you can hear. They can be loud or subtle.

Example: "I hear the hum of the computer, birds chirping outside, and the sound of my breathing."

Notice two things you can smell. If you can't detect any scents, recall two of your favorite smells.

Example: "I smell the aroma of coffee and the fresh scent of my hand lotion."

Focus on one thing you can taste. If you're not eating or drinking, notice the lingering taste in your mouth or recall a favorite flavor.

Example: "I taste the minty freshness of my toothpaste."

Reflect and Breathe

After engaging all five senses, take a moment to notice how you feel. Are you more grounded and present? Do you feel calmer?

Take a few more deep breaths to reinforce your connection to the present moment.

Duration: This exercise typically takes about 5 to 10 minutes and can be practiced anytime you feel the need to reconnect with the present moment.

Case Study: Cultivating Mindfulness Through Nature Walks

- **Participants:** A group of ten individuals aged 25–45, consisting of professionals dealing with high-stress jobs and personal challenges.

- **Objective:** To explore how connecting with nature can enhance mindfulness and promote a greater sense of presence in their daily lives.

- **Method:** The participants engaged in weekly nature walks for over a month, each walk lasting about an hour. They were encouraged to leave their devices behind and focus on the environment around them.

Procedure

1. **Preparation:** Before the first walk, participants attended a brief workshop on mindfulness, discussing its benefits and techniques.

2. **Walk Structure:** Each walk began with a 5-minute guided meditation focusing on breathing and setting intentions for the experience. Participants were reminded to observe their surroundings mindfully.

3. **Observation Prompts:** During the walk, participants were encouraged to identify sensory experiences:

    - What sounds do you hear (birds, rustling leaves)?
    - What colors do you see in the environment?
    - What textures are present (bark, grass, rocks)?

4. **Reflection:** After each walk, participants gathered for a 15-minute discussion to share their experiences and insights, emphasizing feelings of relaxation and connection to the present moment.

Results

- Participants reported heightened awareness of their surroundings, noticing details they had previously overlooked, such as the intricate patterns of leaves and the sound of the wind.

- Many noted significant reductions in stress and anxiety levels, attributing this to the calming effects of nature and the practice of mindfulness.

- Individuals expressed feelings of gratitude and contentment after each walk, which led to an improved overall mood and a sense of connection to both themselves and the world around them.

- Following the study, several participants continued to incorporate nature walks into their routines, with many reporting ongoing benefits for their mental health and mindfulness.

***

It's clear how tuning into our bodies and breathing can enrich our daily experiences. Practices like yoga, tai chi, and even simple posture adjustments offer daily opportunities to cultivate mindfulness. Listening to these subtle cues from our bodies enhances the connection between the mind and body and equips us with tools to navigate life's challenges with greater ease and grace.

Breathing, an often-overlooked yet vital anchor, provides a steadfast pathway to the present amid life's chaos. Through techniques such as breathing, we've seen how intentional focus on our breath fosters relaxation and emotional clarity. It doesn't matter whether you're embracing the vibrancy of nature, enjoying a moment of gratitude, or simply engaging in routine activities; these mindfulness practices build resilience and well-being.

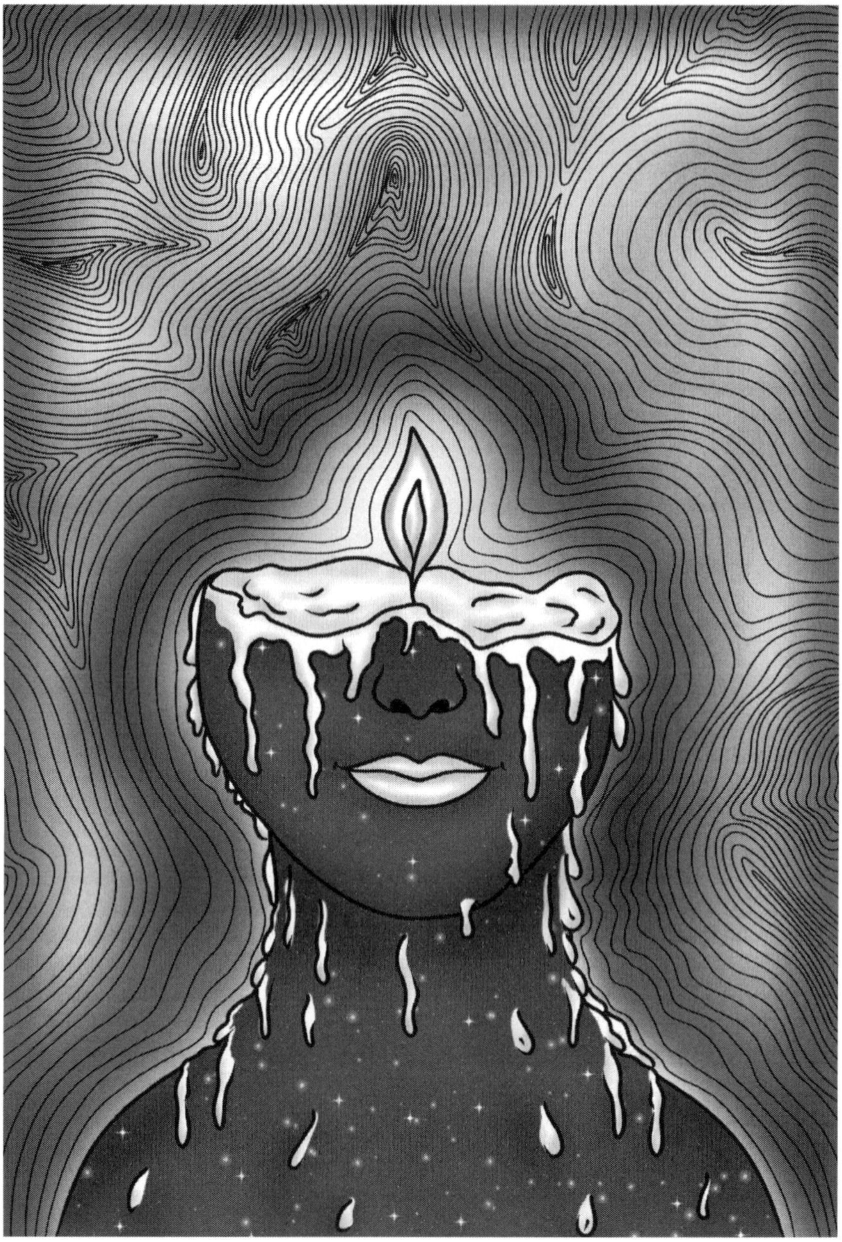

Chapter 6

Observing Without Judgement

If you are at peace, you are living in the present. –Lao Tzu

Scroll through social media, and you'll see it everywhere—opinions flying, judgments being passed, and people eager to weigh in on everything from world events to the latest viral trend.

Everyone wants to be heard, to validate their perspective, or to spark a reaction. But what if, instead of rushing to judge or respond, we simply observed? What if, instead of immediately labeling experiences as good or bad, right or wrong, we simply took the time to observe?

You can watch your thoughts and emotions with curiosity instead of criticism. Instead of beating yourself up for feeling anxious or for overthinking something, you simply acknowledge it—"Oh, I'm feeling this way right now"—without piling on guilt or self-doubt.

This allows us to step back, take in the moment, and truly see things as they are, not as our biases or emotions color them. It's a practice that fosters clarity, patience, and a deeper understanding of the world around us. This shift in perspective transforms how we engage with life.

While judgment and observation may seem similar, they lead to different paths. Judgment filters reality through our personal biases, past experiences, and societal conditioning. It boxes things into categories—"good," "bad," "annoying," and "rude"—often without a deeper understanding.

For example, if an individual responds tersely to a question, a judgmental reaction might label them as rude or unfriendly. However, instead of assuming this, you can simply observe the tension in their body and the hurried pace of their speech—clues that they might be stressed rather than intentionally dismissive, which fosters empathy and clarity.

Observation, on the other hand, is neutral and expansive. It allows us to witness moments as they unfold without inserting our interpretations. For instance, you can watch a scene in a film without analyzing motives or assigning blame; instead, you simply take in the expressions, movements, and dialogue. Let's examine each of these elements in detail.

The Nature of Judgment

Judgment, whether directed towards oneself or others, creates mental clutter and hinders mindfulness by fostering a constant stream of evaluative thoughts and emotional reactions. Here's how this process unfolds and its impact on mindfulness:

- **Creates Mental Noise:** Judgment involves labeling experiences, people, or situations as "good" or "bad," "right" or "wrong." These labels generate a continuous internal dialogue that distracts from the present moment. This mental chatter fills the mind with unnecessary thoughts, making it difficult to focus on what is happening here and now.

- **Reinforces Attachment to Outcomes:** When we judge, we often attach ourselves to specific outcomes or expectations. This attachment creates anxiety about the future or regret about the past, pulling us away from the present moment. Mindfulness, on the other hand, involves accepting things as they are without clinging to desired results or resisting unwanted ones.

- **Triggers Emotional Reactivity:** Judgment often evokes emotions like frustration, anger, guilt, or shame. These emotions can dominate our mental space, making it harder to maintain a calm and clear mind. Emotional reactivity keeps us trapped in cycles of rumination, further cluttering the mind and distancing us from mindfulness.

- **Narrows Perspective:** Judgment tends to create a binary view of the world, where things are seen in black-and-white terms. This limits our ability to perceive the richness and complexity of the present moment. Conversely, mindfulness encourages openness and curiosity, allowing us to experience life in its full spectrum without reducing it to simplistic judgments.

- **Feeds the Ego:** Judgment often stems from the ego's need to assert superiority, control, or self-importance. This reinforces a sense of separation from others and the world, which is antithetical to mindfulness. The latter involves letting go of the ego's demands and connecting with a deeper sense of interconnectedness and presence.

- **Blocks Acceptance:** Judgment is inherently critical and resistant to what is. It creates a barrier to accepting reality as it unfolds, which is a cornerstone of mindfulness. When we constantly evaluate and reject aspects of our experience, we hinder our ability to fully engage with the present moment.

- **Leads to Overthinking:** Judgment often spirals into overthinking as we analyze, compare, and critique our experiences or actions. This overthinking consumes mental energy and keeps us trapped in our heads rather than being present. Mindfulness encourages a state of "being" rather than "thinking," allowing us to experience life directly without excessive mental interference.

Transforming Stressful Moments Through Observation

Consider how this approach can reshape daily frustrations in case you're caught in situations like these:

- **Traffic jam?** Instead of labeling it as an irritating inconvenience, notice the patterns of brake lights, the rhythm of passing cars, and the feel of your breath.

- **Waiting in line?** Observe the people around you—their expressions, their conversations—without forming opinions about them.

- **A difficult conversation?** Instead of crafting a response in your head while the other person is speaking, practice truly listening—absorbing their words, tone, and emotions without rushing to judge or react.

When we observe without judgment, we remove the weight of expectation. The situation remains the same, but our experience of it softens.

How to Cultivate Nonjudgmental Awareness

Here are some simple ways to integrate it into daily life:

Mindful Awareness in Routine Activities: The next time you eat a meal, focus entirely on the experience—the texture, the temperature, and the flavors—without evaluating whether it's the "best" or "worst" you've had. When walking, notice how the ground feels beneath your feet, the movement of air on your skin, and the sounds around you.

Pause Before Reacting: Before forming an opinion about a situation, take a breath. Ask yourself, "Am I observing, or am I judging?" This moment of reflection can create a significant shift in perspective.

Self-Compassion and Reflection: At the end of the day, reflect on moments when judgment arose. Instead of criticizing yourself, view it as an opportunity to learn. How might observation have changed the experience?

Engage in Active Listening: In conversations, resist the urge to immediately analyze or respond. Focus on understanding what is being said, the emotions behind the words, and the silences in between.

Over time, what once felt like an obligation to critique transforms into a state of presence and acceptance that enriches our personal lives as well as our relationships. I don't mean that you become passive simply because you are observing. You are meeting life as it is, moment by moment, without the extra weight of unnecessary labels.

Use the "Just Noticing" Technique: Mentally note what is happening in the moment. For instance, you can say, *"I'm just noticing stress."* or *"I'm just noticing my rapid heartbeat."* That helps you stay present and prevents you from getting caught up in the story behind the stress.

Use Neutral Language: Replace judgmental or evaluative language with neutral, observational phrases. For example: Instead of, *"This is terrible,"* say, *"This is happening."* Instead of, *"I don't like this,"* say, *"I notice discomfort."* This shifts your focus from evaluation to simple awareness.

Techniques for Observing Without Judgment

It's possible to train ourselves to observe without immediate judgment. Through these simple yet powerful techniques, we can gradually reframe our thoughts, regulate our emotions, and cultivate a more balanced way of engaging with life.

Cognitive reframing: This practice shifts negative interpretations into neutral, fact-based observations. Consider this scenario: You have an important presentation coming up, and you feel anxious. A judgmental response might be:

- *I'm terrible at public speaking. I always get nervous, and it's going to go badly.*

Now, let's reframe it into an observation:

- *I notice my heart beating faster and thoughts racing as I prepare for my presentation. My body is responding to a challenge.*

Instead of being overwhelmed by emotions, you acknowledge them as natural physiological reactions. This neutral perspective creates mental space for rational thinking and emotional regulation, making it easier to respond thoughtfully rather than react impulsively.

Throughout the day, take note of any negative or judgmental thoughts. Instead of labeling them as "bad" or resisting them, try to describe them objectively, as if you were an outside observer. With time, this practice retrains your mind to approach experiences with openness rather than assumptions.

Mindful Breathing: Judgment often arises when our minds drift—either reliving past experiences or anticipating the future. Mindful breathing brings us back to the present, preventing unnecessary mental narratives from taking over. Consider this: Each time your thoughts wander toward judgment—whether about yourself, others, or a situation—gently return to your breath. Breathing with intention shifts focus from critical thoughts to simple presence. Over time, this practice fosters a habit of observing without attaching a story to what arises. You can apply all the other practical tips from the previous chapters.

Training the Mind to Observe: Sometimes, our minds need a mental rehearsal to break habitual patterns of judgment. Guided imagery is a powerful technique that helps us practice observation in a relaxed, controlled environment.

You can imagine yourself walking through a peaceful forest or along a quiet beach. As you move through this scene, focus on purely observing—the colors, textures, sounds, and sensations—without labeling anything as "good" or "bad." This practice conditions the mind to engage with experiences without instantly categorizing them. Over time, this habit extends into daily life, making it easier to witness situations without judgment.

Use recorded guided imagery sessions (available online) to deepen this practice. Alternatively, create your own scene and visualize it for a few minutes each day.

Journaling: Writing down our thoughts offers a mirror into the mind, revealing recurring judgments and patterns. Journaling is an effective way to become more aware of our internal dialogue and gradually shift from criticism to observation. Instead of writing how you feel about a situation, try writing what you notice about it. For example, rather than:

- *I was so awkward in that conversation today. I shouldn't have said that.*

Reframe it as:

- *During today's conversation, I noticed moments where I hesitated before speaking. I felt a tightness in my chest, and my mind raced afterward.*

Dedicate a few minutes each day to freewriting. Don't filter or analyze—just let your thoughts flow onto the page without judgment. Over time, you'll notice shifts in how you perceive yourself and your experiences.

How These Techniques Work Together

Each of these practices builds upon the others:

- **Reframing thoughts** reduces emotional reactivity.

- **Mindful breathing** strengthens present-moment awareness.

- **Guided imagery** trains the mind to observe neutrally.

- **Journaling** deepens self-reflection and reinforces mindful habits.

Embracing Imperfection

Perfection is often upheld as the ultimate goal—whether in work, relationships, or personal pursuits. We are conditioned to believe that flawless execution equates to success and that mistakes signal failure. Yet, this pursuit of perfection can create unnecessary stress, self-doubt, and fear of failure, ultimately limiting our growth and creativity.

Imperfection doesn't mean that we settle for mediocrity; rather, it invites us to recognize the beauty and value in the imperfect, the unfinished, and the evolving. It is an invitation to step away from rigid expectations and into a more authentic, compassionate, and fulfilling way of living.

What if the very things we perceive as imperfections are what make us unique, relatable, and deeply human? It's relieving to acknowledge that it's okay not to have everything figured out. Life involves learning, adapting, and growing, and imperfection is not a barrier to success but a pathway to it. When we redefine perfection in this way:

- Stress levels decrease, as we no longer feel pressured to meet impossible standards.

- Creativity flourishes because the fear of making mistakes no longer stifles expression.

- Authenticity deepens, as we become more comfortable showing up as we are, rather than hiding behind a façade of flawlessness.

Learn from your failures: To truly embrace imperfection, instead of viewing our mistakes as failures, we can see them as lessons—opportunities to learn, improve, and gain wisdom. For example, if you make a mistake at work, rather than criticizing yourself, ask:

- *What can this experience teach me?*

- *How can I use this to improve?*

That shows self-compassion, which over time this practice softens harsh self-judgment and fosters greater inner peace.

Share Your Imperfections: Engage in conversations where you openly discuss experiences that didn't go as expected.

- Talking about failures normalizes imperfection, making it clear that everyone struggles and learns.

- It builds a supportive, judgment-free environment, fostering deeper connections with others.

Use Art as an Expression of Imperfection: Artistic pursuits—whether painting, writing, music, or photography can help you celebrate imperfections.

- Create without the pressure of meeting a standard. Let go of expectations and allow flaws to be part of the process.

- This mindset enhances self-acceptance and encourages seeing the beauty in the imperfect—both in yourself and the world around you.

***

When we observe without judgment, we cultivate a deeper connection to the present moment. This enhances our ability to respond to challenges with wisdom and equanimity. Over time, this practice becomes a powerful tool for self-awareness, emotional resilience, and personal growth. We invite a more compassionate and authentic way of being and unlock the true essence of mindfulness: a profound sense of presence, acceptance, and inner peace that eventually allows us to take control of our emotions. We will discuss that next.

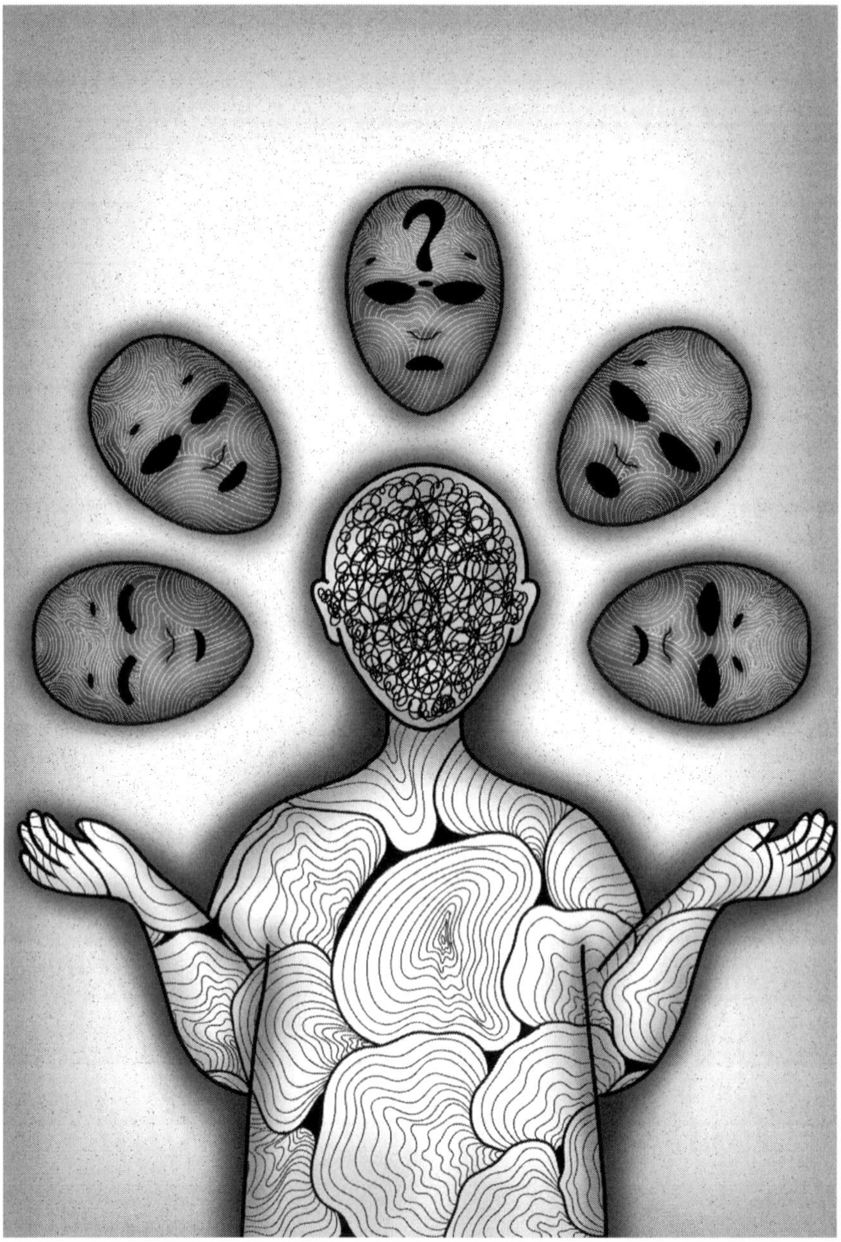

Chapter 7

Developing Emotional Awareness

Realize deeply that the present moment is all you ever have.
–Eckhart Tolle

When Richard first embarked on a journey to master his emotions, he realized how easy it was to overlook the multitude of emotions we experience daily. Beyond knowing a handful of emotions like anger, happiness, sadness, and excitement, he discovered that they shape our experiences, influence our choices, and guide how we connect with others.

Richard discovered that emotions aren't just feelings that come and go; they move us. Think about it—when you're inspired, you take action. When you're frustrated, you might withdraw or react. When you're anxious, you might avoid social interactions. If you're happy, you're open to new experiences; if you're stressed, you might be irritable, which affects how you interact with others.

Every emotion carries energy and purpose, and when we become more aware of them, we can better understand what drives us and what holds us back.

Emotions have stories, patterns, and even physical sensations tied to them. When you feel anxious, your body tenses up. When you feel joy, your breath becomes lighter. Recognizing these signals helps us become more present, more attuned to ourselves, and more intentional in how we respond to life.

That's why emotional awareness matters. It's not about labeling emotions as "good" or "bad." We get to understand and allow them to guide us without overwhelming us. And what is the best way to do that? Curiosity. When you approach your emotions with curiosity instead of judgment, you open yourself up to growth, self-acceptance, and new possibilities that you might not have seen before.

Naming your emotions can reduce their intensity and help you understand what is triggering them. If stress makes you short-tempered, for instance, understanding this connection helps you address the root cause rather than simply reacting out of frustration. Over time, this awareness fosters healthier relationships and better decision-making.

In other cases, you might find quiet satisfaction in daily moments, such as the comfort of a familiar routine. As you become more attuned to your emotions, you develop a deeper connection with your true self, leading to personal growth and greater well-being. Emotions are signals that inform us about our environment and our reactions to it.

Here are a few ways to acknowledge your emotions without being overwhelmed by them:

1. **Observe Your Emotions:** Instead of getting caught up in your emotions, try to observe them as if you were an outsider. Notice how they manifest in your body and mind. Does your heart race when you're anxious? Observing can create a space between you and your emotions, giving you more control over your reactions.

2. **Don't Identify With Your Emotions:** Remember that you are not your emotions. You experience emotions, but they do not define you. This perspective can help you avoid being overwhelmed by them.

3. **Develop Emotional Regulation Skills:** Techniques such as deep breathing, meditation, or progressive muscle relaxation can help you manage the physiological aspects of your emotions and prevent them from escalating.

4. **Practice Self-Compassion:** Be kind to yourself. Understand that everyone experiences difficult emotions, and it's okay to not be okay sometimes. Self-compassion can help you recover from emotional setbacks more quickly.

The Connection Between Thoughts and Emotions

The interplay between thoughts and emotions is a powerful dynamic that shapes our perception of the world. Our thoughts can either intensify or soothe emotions, influencing how we feel and react. Consider these two perspectives on the same situation:

- Telling yourself, *I am capable,* during a stressful moment can boost your confidence and ease anxiety.

- Thinking, *I always mess up,* in a similar situation can heighten frustration and self-doubt.

By becoming conscious of our cognitive patterns, we gain the ability to shift our mindset toward more positive, constructive narratives. This skill is crucial for emotional regulation, transforming distress into opportunities for growth.

How Mindfulness Improves Emotional Awareness

Mindfulness can help you stay grounded in the present moment. You are less likely to get caught up in the stories your mind tells you about your emotions, which can amplify them. It can significantly contribute to building resilience and reducing emotional reactivity.

Here's how:

1. **Enhanced Awareness:** Mindfulness encourages individuals to become more aware of their thoughts, emotions, and bodily sensations. This heightened awareness can help people recognize when they begin to feel overwhelmed or reactive, allowing them to pause and choose a more thoughtful response.

2. **Emotional Regulation:** Regular mindfulness practice helps individuals develop better emotional regulation skills. By observing their emotions without judgment, practitioners can create a space between their feelings and reactions, reducing impulsive responses to stressors.

3. **Stress Reduction:** Mindfulness has been shown to lower levels of stress by promoting relaxation and reducing anxiety. When stress levels decrease, individuals are less likely to react emotionally to challenging situations, leading to more grounded and resilient responses.

4. **Improved Focus and Clarity:** Mindfulness enhances cognitive functions such as focus and clarity of thought. With a clearer mind, individuals can approach problems more effectively, reducing the likelihood of feeling overwhelmed and reactive when faced with challenges.

5. **Positive Perspective:** Mindfulness fosters a more positive outlook on life by encouraging gratitude and acceptance. This shift in perspective can help individuals cope with adversity more effectively, enhancing resilience by helping them see challenges as opportunities for growth.

6. **Connection and Empathy:** Practicing mindfulness can improve interpersonal relationships by enhancing empathy and understanding. Strong social support is a key factor in resilience, as it allows individuals to navigate difficult emotions and situations more effectively.

7. **Behavioral Responses:** By cultivating mindfulness, individuals can learn to respond to emotional triggers with intention rather than automatic reactions. This ability to respond mindfully can lead to healthier interactions and decision-making, ultimately contributing to resilience.

Recognizing Emotional Triggers

Understanding our emotional triggers is a crucial step toward self-awareness and emotional regulation. Emotional triggers are specific situations, events, or interactions that provoke intense emotional responses, often stemming from past experiences or deeply ingrained beliefs. Recognizing these triggers allows us to respond thoughtfully, thereby creating greater emotional balance.

To uncover them, begin by observing your emotional reactions throughout the day. Notice moments when your emotions feel disproportionately intense compared to the situation at hand—these are often clues pointing to an underlying trigger.

Common emotional triggers might include:

- Certain topics of conversation (e.g., discussions about success, relationships, or personal failures).
- Specific environments (e.g., crowded spaces, workplaces, or family gatherings).
- Interactions with particular individuals (e.g., criticism from a boss or comments from a family member).

Once you've identified the triggers, analyze how you react to them. Many of us develop habitual emotional responses, such as:

- Withdrawing or shutting down during conflicts.
- Becoming defensive when receiving criticism.
- Reacting with frustration when we feel unheard.

After an emotional experience, take some time to reflect on it. What can you learn from it? How can you handle a similar situation better in the future? Are there patterns in how you respond? Understanding these tendencies allows you to break negative emotional cycles and replace them with more constructive reactions.

Journaling for Emotional Clarity

Keeping an emotional journal can help identify recurring themes in your emotional responses. For example, if you often feel frustrated after work meetings, your journal may reveal that your triggers are:

- Being interrupted while speaking.
- Feeling dismissed or undervalued.

Journaling acts as a mirror to your inner world, providing clarity on emotional triggers and helping you respond with greater awareness over time.

The Power of Communication

Discussing emotional triggers with trusted individuals—friends, family, or mental health professionals—can lessen their impact. Verbalizing your emotions can:

- Reduce their intensity.

- Foster empathy and understanding in relationships.

- Provide new perspectives on handling triggers.

However, sharing vulnerabilities takes courage. Choose people who will respond with compassion and understanding. Thoughtful communication can transform how you perceive your triggers, making them feel more manageable and less overwhelming.

Creating a Supportive Environment

To manage emotional triggers effectively, establish safe spaces where you feel comfortable expressing emotions without fear of judgment. These can be:

- Physical spaces, like a quiet room for reflection.
- Emotional spaces, such as conversations with a supportive friend.

To proactively manage your triggers, consider these steps:

1. Develop mindfulness habits: Regular self-awareness practices help recognize triggers early.
2. Approach with curiosity, not judgment: Ask, *Why does this provoke such a strong response?*
3. Create personalized coping mechanisms, for example:
   - Pausing before reacting.
   - Using grounding techniques (e.g., focusing on your breath, touching a familiar object).
   - Channeling emotions into creative outlets (e.g., art, journaling, or movement).

By incorporating these tools into your daily life, you can transform emotional triggers from obstacles into opportunities for self-growth.

Practicing the RAIN Technique

The RAIN technique, a structured approach to processing emotions with care and understanding, consists of four steps: Recognize, Allow, Investigate, and Nurture.

Recognize: Acknowledge Your Emotions

Recognize what you are feeling. Many of us instinctively avoid unpleasant emotions, distracting ourselves instead of confronting them. However, suppressing emotions often amplifies their intensity over time.

Instead, acknowledging emotions helps dismantle avoidance behaviors. For example, if you feel irritation during a hectic day, simply recognizing it as a signal from within brings awareness without an immediate reaction.

Allow: Make Space for Emotions

Once we recognize an emotion, we allow it to exist without resistance. Our natural impulse might be to push stress or anxiety away, but emotions tend to persist when ignored.

Allowing emotions is like observing a storm—you don't try to stop it; instead, you acknowledge that it will pass. Rather than fighting emotions, sit with them briefly, noticing their nuances without judgment. Over time, this practice reduces emotional intensity and promotes acceptance.

Investigate: Explore with Curiosity

This investigative step encourages self-inquiry rather than self-judgment. Ask yourself:

- *Why am I feeling this way?*

- *What triggered this reaction?*

- *How does this emotion influence my thoughts and actions?*

This process is akin to exploring hidden landscapes within yourself, uncovering patterns and beliefs that shape your responses. For instance, persistent anxiety may stem from a childhood fear of failure. Understanding these connections empowers you to respond thoughtfully rather than react impulsively.

Nurture: Cultivate Self-Compassion

The final step, nurture, reminds us to treat ourselves with kindness, especially when our emotions feel overwhelming. Life's challenges are inevitable, but how we respond to them shapes our personal growth.

Self-compassionate practices include:

- Reflecting on past successes.

- Seeking support from loved ones.

- Engaging in soothing activities such as journaling or meditation.

This step is where healing begins—where setbacks become stepping stones instead of stumbling blocks.

Each element of the RAIN technique contributes uniquely to emotional intelligence in the following ways:

- Recognizing emotions fosters self-discovery.

- Allowing emotions reduces resistance and stress.

- Investigating emotions deepens understanding.

- Nurturing yourself builds resilience and promotes personal growth.

Resilience is strengthened not just individually but also collectively. When we connect with others on similar journeys, we create a network of support. Our relationships reinforce emotional strength. Whether through mindfulness groups, supportive conversations, or shared experiences, these connections cultivate a sense of belonging and mutual encouragement.

***

Understanding our emotions helps us navigate life with greater self-awareness and growth. Mindfulness practices, such as the RAIN technique and resilience-building strategies, allow us to engage with our emotions without fear or judgment.

Integrating these practices into our daily lives offers stability amidst uncertainty. Whether you're seeking calm, clarity, or deeper self-understanding, mindfulness provides a guiding light on your journey toward emotional well-being. Through awareness, acceptance, and self-compassion, you cultivate a more balanced, resilient, and fulfilling life.

Emotional Awareness Worksheet

Objective: To enhance emotional awareness by identifying, understanding, and managing emotions effectively.

Part 1: Identifying Emotions

1. **Emotion Identification**

    o List five emotions you have experienced in the past week.

    a.

    b.

    c.

    d.

    e.

2. **Emotion Triggers**

    o   For each emotion listed above, identify what triggered it.

    a. Emotion:

    b. Trigger:

    c. Emotion:

    d. Trigger:

    e. Emotion:

    f. Trigger:

    g. Emotion:

    h. Trigger:

    i. Emotion:

    j. Trigger:

Part 2: Understanding Emotions

3. **Physical Sensations**

    o   Describe the physical sensations you associate with each emotion.

    a. Emotion:

    b. Sensations:

    c. Emotion:

    d. Sensations:

    e. Emotion:

    f. Sensations:

    g. Emotion:

    h. Sensations:

i. Emotion:

j. Sensations:

4. **Thought Patterns**

    o   What thoughts accompany each emotion?

    a. Emotion:

    b. Thoughts:

    c. Emotion:

    d. Thoughts:

    e. Emotion:

    f. Thoughts:

    g. Emotion:

    h. Thoughts:

Part 3: Managing Emotions

5. **Coping Strategies**

    o   List 3 healthy coping strategies you can use when experiencing strong emotions.

    a.

    b.

    c.

6. **Emotion Regulation**

    o   Choose one emotion from your list and describe how you can regulate it.

    o   Emotion:

    o   Regulation Strategy:

Part 4: Reflecting on Emotions

7. **Emotional Patterns**
    - Reflect on any patterns you notice in your emotions and triggers.
    - Pattern:
    - Possible Cause:

8. **Emotional Growth**
    - What is one step you can take to improve your emotional awareness?
    - Step:

Part 5: Daily Emotional Check-In

9. **Daily Check-In**
    - At the end of each day, take a few minutes to reflect on your emotions.
    - Today, I felt:
    - The main trigger was:
    - How I handled it:
    - What I can improve:

Regularly completing this worksheet can help you become more attuned to your emotions, understand their origins, and develop healthier ways to manage them.

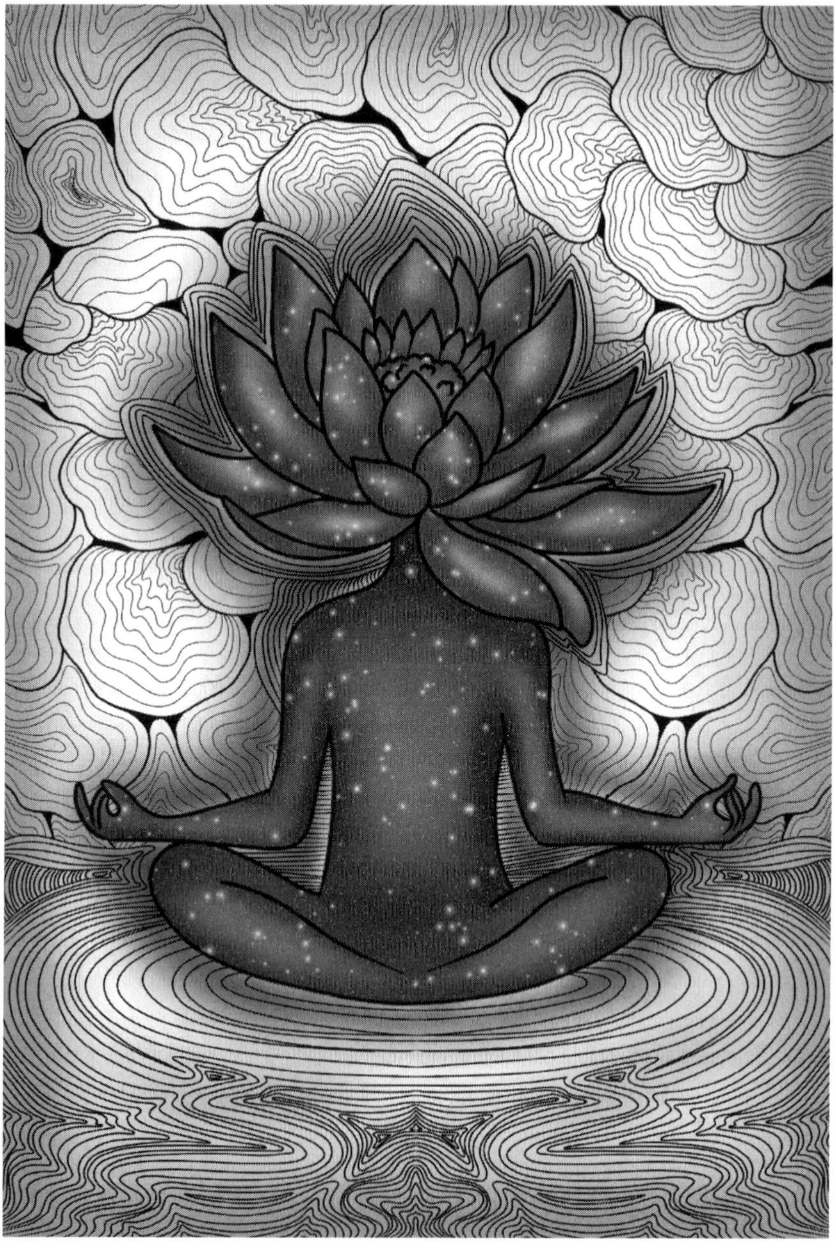

Chapter 8

Sustaining Mindfulness in Everyday Life

Do not dwell in the past, do not dream of the future, concentrate the mind on the present moment. –Buddha

From the moment you wake up until you settle into bed, there are countless opportunities to pause, breathe, and be present. These shifts can transform routine moments into sources of calm and clarity.

Mornings set the tone for everything that follows. Instead of rushing straight into the day, what if you took just a moment to pause? Before even getting out of bed, take a deep breath. Notice how the air fills your lungs and how your body gently wakes up. This single breath can become the first mindful moment of your day.

If mornings feel hectic, start small. Perhaps it's sipping your coffee or tea without distractions. Perhaps it's stretching gently and noticing how your muscles feel as they awaken. You don't need a 30-minute meditation session—just a few mindful moments to ground yourself before the day pulls you in different directions.

Another simple practice is setting an intention. Instead of letting the day run on autopilot, take a moment to ask yourself:

How do I want to show up today?

Your intention could be as simple as "stay patient" or "listen more." Writing it down or repeating it in your mind helps keep it in focus.

Mindful Breaks

We all experience moments when we feel drained, distracted, or overwhelmed. That's where mindful breaks come in. Let's say you've been staring at a screen for hours and your focus is slipping. Instead of pushing through, try stepping away for a minute. Look out the window and take in what you see—the colors, the movement of the trees, and the way the light shifts. Alternatively, just close your eyes and take a few deep breaths, allowing your body to relax with each exhale.

Gratitude is another powerful reset. When you pause, take a moment to appreciate something—maybe a kind message from a friend, the taste of your lunch, or even just the feeling of stretching after sitting for too long. It doesn't have to be profound; even the smallest moments of gratitude can shift your mindset.

These breaks don't have to be long. A minute or two is enough to refresh your mind and bring you back to the present.

Ending the Day With Reflection

At night, instead of letting the day blur into sleep, take a moment to reflect. Ask yourself: *What was one good thing that happened today?* Perhaps it was a smile from a stranger, finishing a task, or simply getting through a tough moment.

Journaling can help, too. It doesn't have to be a long entry—just a few lines about something you learned, felt grateful for, or want to improve. Over time, these small reflections can help you notice patterns, celebrate progress, and bring more awareness to your daily life.

Some days can be tough but remember that the goal is to meet each day with curiosity and kindness, learning from both the good and the challenging moments.

Bringing Mindfulness Into Everyday Activities

Mindfulness can be part of what you are already doing. Here's how:

1. **Mindful Communication**

Instead of just hearing words, truly listen. Whether you are talking with a friend, family member, or colleague, try to be fully present. Put down your phone, make eye contact, and take in what they are saying without planning your response. This simple shift can deepen relationships and reduce misunderstandings.

2. **Mindful Eating**

We often eat while multitasking—scrolling, watching TV, or rushing through a meal. The next time you eat, try slowing down. Notice the colors, textures, and flavors of your food. Chew slowly and appreciate the nourishment. Not only does this enhance the experience, but it also helps you recognize when you are full, improving both digestion and enjoyment.

3. **Mindful Movement**

Exercise is not only about burning calories; it is also a chance to connect with your body. Whether it is yoga, a walk, or stretching, focus on how your body feels. Notice your breath, the way your muscles engage, and the rhythm of movement. This transforms movement into a stress reliever rather than just another task on your list.

4. **Mindful Technology Use**

We are constantly bombarded by notifications, emails, and endless scrolling. Try setting small boundaries—for example, no phones during meals or a tech-free hour before bed. Notice how you feel when you step away from screens for a bit. Creating these mindful pauses can help reduce stress and improve focus.

Even routine tasks can become mindful moments. Instead of rushing through chores, try fully engaging with them:

- **Brushing your teeth:** Feel the bristles, taste the toothpaste, and notice the motion.

- **Showering:** Pay attention to the warmth of the water, the scent of the soap, and the sensation of lathering.

- **Cooking:** Listen to the sizzle of the food, smell the spices, and feel the textures.

- **Commuting:** Instead of zoning out, notice your surroundings, breathe deeply, or fully enjoy the music.

From Fear to Freedom: Mindfulness Changed My Destiny

As told by Janet

From a young age, I carried a heavy weight of fear and anxiety that seemed to follow me everywhere. During my childhood, I was filled with a constant sense of dread. I was afraid of almost everything—going to sleep, being away from my mother, and even the simplest daily activities felt overwhelming. The world felt like a dangerous place, and I was always bracing for the worst.

School was a particular challenge. The thought of being surrounded by unfamiliar children made my chest tighten and my stomach churn. I didn't want to ride in cars with too many people because I was convinced the car would break down. Boats terrified me—what if they capsized? Even being at home with a babysitter was unbearable because I was certain my mother wouldn't return. My mind was a whirlwind of catastrophic thoughts: *What if I get lost? What if I end up in the hospital? What if I'm separated from my family? What if I die?* These fears kept me in a constant state of high alert, as though I were always waiting for disaster to strike."

Anxiety became my shadow, following me into adulthood. I sought therapy at various points in my life—first as a child, then as a student, and later as a young adult. While therapy helped reduce the intensity of my anxiety, it never fully went away. It lingered, a quiet but persistent hum in the background of my life.

Everything changed when I discovered mindfulness in my late 30s. At first, I was skeptical. How could something as simple as paying attention to the present moment make a difference? But as I began to practice—sitting quietly, focusing on my breath, and observing my thoughts without judgment—I started to notice subtle shifts. I came to understand that my anxiety wasn't just a random affliction; it was rooted in my early experiences.

Having lost my father as a child, my mother raised my siblings and me as a single parent. She worked long hours to provide for us, and while she did her best, I often felt alone and unsafe. I learned to be self-reliant at a young age, but that independence came at a cost. I never felt truly secure, and that lack of safety manifested as constant worry and fear.

Mindfulness didn't erase those early experiences, but it helped me see them in a new light. By observing my thoughts and emotions without getting caught up in them, I began to understand that my anxiety was a response to past experiences, not a reflection of present reality. This awareness allowed me to approach myself with compassion rather than criticism. Instead of fighting my anxiety, I learned to acknowledge it, to sit with it, and to let it pass without allowing it to define me.

Over time, mindfulness has taught me how to ground myself in the present moment, recognize when my mind is spiraling into catastrophic thinking, and gently guide myself back to the here and now. I have started to notice the beauty in small, everyday moments—the warmth of sunlight on my skin, the sound of birds chirping, and the feeling of my breath moving in and out. These moments have helped me feel more connected and less afraid.

Today, anxiety no longer controls my life. It still visits from time to time, but I have learned how to meet it with kindness and curiosity rather than fear. Mindfulness has given me the tools to navigate life's challenges with greater ease and resilience. I have found a sense of peace and safety within myself—something I never thought possible.

Conclusion

It is possible to live a peaceful, thriving life both physically and emotionally, even amid the inevitable stresses of modern living. Through the mindful steps explored in this book, you now possess the tools to cast off the weight of negativity, stress, self-criticism, and the relentless grip of bodily discomfort.

You no longer need to be a prisoner of the past or a hostage to the future. You have learned how to interrupt invasive thought patterns, creating space for moments of calm to take root and flourish.

You've discovered that noticing your thoughts without being enslaved by them unlocks transformative power. For instance, practicing labeling your thoughts, such as "This is stress" or "Here's self-criticism again," creates a subtle but powerful distance between you and your inner narratives.

When mistakes happen or poor decisions are made, you now know that self-compassion is your gentle ally. You've learned to offer yourself affirmations soaked in tenderness and have practiced loving-kindness meditations that embrace both your flaws and strengths. Silencing your inner critic is not an overnight task, but each time you redirect self-talk toward compassion, you strengthen your resilience. Over time, this practice becomes second nature, and the voice of self-judgment grows quieter, replaced by a kinder, more supportive inner dialogue.

You now appreciate the value of tuning into the present moment more than ever. The practice, as you've discovered, forges a deeper connection between your mind and body. How? Grounding techniques like mindful breathing and body scans have become your tools for staying centered. You've learned to savor even the simplest experiences, transforming the mundane into the extraordinary. A cup of tea becomes a meditation; a walk in the park is a serene exploration of sensations; and a quiet moment at home is an opportunity for reflection.

You've learned to observe life without the incessant judgment that once clouded your perspective. By moving from labeling experiences as "good" or "bad" to simply observing them as they are, you release yourself from the shackles of perfectionism.

Life's imperfections no longer have to feel like burdens but rather invitations to embrace reality as it unfolds. As a result, you're kinder and more open-hearted to both the world and yourself.

You are better positioned to manage your emotions because you now understand their role and have learned to acknowledge them without becoming overwhelmed by their intensity. Techniques like RAIN—Recognize, Allow, Investigate, Nurture—have become your guideposts for processing emotions mindfully.

Finally, I pray that you do not leave mindfulness behind. Weave it into the fabric of your daily life. Transform what once felt like ordinary, overlooked moments into opportunities for presence and connection.

Let eating become a meditation, walking be a mindful exploration of movement, and driving a chance for quiet reflection. These consistent practices extend beyond structured sessions, enriching your life with depth, authenticity, and a profound sense of aliveness.

While this journey is not without its challenges, do not let the fluctuations become obstacles; they are part of the mosaic of life. Let each experience become an opportunity to practice mindfulness.

And so, dear reader, when stress tries to ensnare you and overthinking threatens your peace, remember the power of awareness, the balm of self-compassion, and the grounding force of the present moment. Carry these practices with you, nurture them, and watch as they unfold into a more mindful way of being.

May your path be one of lightness and curiosity, where each moment brings you closer to a profound connection with yourself and the world around you. Welcome to the journey of living mindfully.

Glossary

5-4-3-2-1 Exercise: A grounding technique that utilizes the five senses to anchor an individual in the present moment.

Active Listening: Fully focusing on and understanding what someone is saying without the urge to immediately respond or judge.

Affirmations: Positive statements that help challenge and overcome negative thoughts and self-doubt.

Avoidance: A coping mechanism involving avoiding stress-inducing situations, which can increase anxiety in the long run.

Balloon Release Technique: A visualization where thoughts are imagined as balloons that can be released to help let go of them.

Black-and-White Thinking: Viewing situations in extremes without recognizing middle ground.

Body Awareness: Recognizing bodily sensations and feelings to promote grounding and connection to the present.

Body Scan Techniques: Practices that increase awareness of physical sensations and tensions in the body, helping to release stress.

Boundaries: Limits set in relationships to protect emotional and mental well-being.

Cognitive Appraisal: The process of interpreting and evaluating stressors, which influences emotional responses.

Cognitive Defusion: Stepping back from thoughts and observing them without emotional entanglement.

Cognitive Habits: Thinking patterns that contribute to overthinking, such as an analytical mindset or high sensitivity.

Cognitive Patterns: Recurrent ways of thinking that influence perceptions and emotional responses.

Cognitive Reframing: Shifting negative interpretations into neutral, fact-based perspectives to reduce distress.

Common Humanity: Recognizing suffering as part of the shared human experience, fostering a sense of connection.

Curiosity: An open-minded and inquisitive approach toward emotions and experiences, promoting self-acceptance.

Default Mode Network (DMN): A part of the brain responsible for self-reflection and daydreaming, which is often overactive in overthinkers.

Depression: A mood disorder marked by persistent sadness and loss of interest, which impacts daily life.

Detaching from Thoughts: Creating space between oneself and thoughts to reduce emotional impact.

Distress: Negative stress that becomes overwhelming and impacts health and emotions.

Emotional Awareness: Recognizing, understanding, and managing one's own emotions, as well as the emotions of others.

Emotional Reactivity: The tendency to have strong emotional responses that can hinder mindfulness.

Emotional Regulation: Managing and responding to emotional experiences effectively.

Emotional Resilience: The ability to adapt to and recover from emotional challenges, enhanced through mindfulness and self-compassion.

Emotional Triggers: Specific events or situations that provoke strong emotional reactions based on past experiences.

Empathy: Understanding and sharing the feelings of another, which fosters deeper connections.

Endocrine System: The hormone-regulating system that can be disrupted by stress, affecting appetite and metabolism.

Eustress: A beneficial form of stress that encourages performance and motivation.

Fear of Uncertainty: Anxiety stemming from a desire for predictability, leading to excessive worry.

Gratitude: A feeling of thankfulness and appreciation for the positive aspects of life.

Grounding Technique: Exercises that help individuals reconnect with the present moment, interrupting spiraling thoughts.

Guided Imagery: A visualization technique that allows individuals to engage with experiences without labeling them.

Inner Critic: The negative internal voice that judges or criticizes oneself, often leading to feelings of inadequacy.

Intrinsic Self-Worth: A sense of worth that is inherent and not dependent on external validation.

Journaling for Clarity: Writing thoughts down to help process and clarify feelings, thereby reducing mental clutter.

Journaling: Writing down thoughts and feelings to gain insights into emotional triggers and patterns.

Loving-Kindness Meditation (Metta): A meditation practice that cultivates feelings of compassion toward oneself and others.

Mental Clutter: The overwhelming feeling of having too many competing thoughts, which makes concentration difficult.

Mental Health: Emotional, psychological, and social well-being that affects how one thinks, feels, and acts.

Mental Noise: The constant stream of thoughts and emotional reactions that distract from the present moment.

Mindful Breaks: Short pauses taken throughout the day to refresh the mind and bring attention back to the present.

Mindful Communication: Engaging fully in conversations by listening attentively and being present.

Mindful Eating: Eating with focus and appreciation while being aware of the flavors, textures, and nutritional value of food.

Mindful Labeling: Differentiating between facts, opinions, and emotions to evaluate thoughts clearly.

Mindful Movement: Engaging in physical activities with a focus on the body's sensations rather than the end goal.

Mindful Technology Use: Setting boundaries on technology use to foster presence and reduce distractions.

Observation: Watching or noticing something without personal interpretation or judgment.

Overgeneralizing: A cognitive distortion in which one failure is seen as evidence of failure in all aspects of life.

Overthinking: The excessive analysis of thoughts or situations that leads to mental exhaustion and anxiety.

Past Trauma: Emotional scars from distressing experiences that influence current thought patterns.

Pause Ritual: A personal practice designed to facilitate regular pauses throughout the day.

Perfectionism: A relentless pursuit of flawlessness, often accompanied by excessive self-criticism.

Progressive Muscle Relaxation: A technique involving tensing and relaxing muscle groups to alleviate physical tension tied to stress.

Resilience: The ability to recover quickly from difficulties and adapt in the face of adversity.

Self-Acceptance: Recognizing and embracing one's strengths and weaknesses without self-judgment.

Self-Care: Activities and practices that maintain and improve well-being.

Self-Compassion: Treating oneself with kindness and understanding during moments of struggle.

Self-Kindness: Offering warmth and understanding to oneself instead of being harshly critical.

Stress: A natural response to perceived threats or demands, which can be physical, emotional, or psychological.

Stressful Life Events: Major life changes that create instability and trigger overthinking.

Supportive Inner Dialogue: A positive and encouraging way of speaking to oneself to counter self-criticism.

The Power of the Pause: Taking a moment to breathe and choose a response instead of reacting impulsively.

The RAIN Technique: A mindfulness method for processing emotions: Recognize, Allow, Investigate, and Nurture.

Thought Labeling: Write down and categorize thoughts to identify themes and reduce their power.

Thought Reframing: Change negative thought patterns into more balanced perspectives.

Thought Train Visualization: Visualize thoughts as passengers on a train, reinforcing their temporary nature.

Three-Breath Pause: Engage in a quick mindfulness exercise to regain composure by taking three deep breaths.

Transition Pauses: Take moments to reset and refocus between different tasks.

Understanding Thought Patterns: Notice recurring thoughts and their triggers to break negative cycles.

References

Address by President John F. Kennedy to UN General Assembly. (1963, September 20). US Department of State. https://2009-2017.state.gov/p/io/potusunga/207201.htm

AJ. (n.d). *245 Quotes by Buddha.* Elevate Society. https://elevatesociety.com/quotes-by-buddha/

Analysis of you can observe a lot by watching someone by Yogi Berra. (n.d). bartlebyresearch. https://www.bartleby.com/essay/Analaysis-Of-You-Can-Observe-A-Lot-9E4A0120AFE64134

Anxiety disorders – Facts & Statistics. (2022, October 10). Anxiety & Depression Association of America. https://adaa.org/umderstanding-anxiety/facts-statistics

Eckhart, T. (n.d). *Eckhart Tolle Quotes.* Goodreads. https://www.goodreads.com/author/quotes/4493.Eckhart_Tolle

Einstein, A. (n.d). *Quote of Albert Einstein.* BrainyQuotes. https://www.brainyquote.com/quotes/albert_einstein_136891

Solomon, D.A. (2023, October 27). *How clutter is killing your mental health.* Galia Collaborative. https://galiacollaborative.com/how-clutter-is-killing-your-mental-health/

How to manage stress with mindfulness and meditation. (n.d). Mindful. https://www.mindful.org/how-to-manage-stress-with-mindfulness-and-meditation/

Kanat, A. (2020, March 30). Buddha says. *Readers' Blog.* https://timesofindia.indiatimes.com/readersblog/kanatsense/buddha-says-11232/

Tzu, L. (n.d). *Quote of Lao Tzu.* Goodreads. https://www.goodreads.com/author/quotes/2622245.Lao_Tzu

10 amazing statistics to celebrate national gratitude month. (2022, October 17). PennState Pro Wellness. https://prowellness.childrens.pennstatehealth.org/10-amazing-statistics-to-celebrate-national-gratitude-month

Marks, H., & King, L. M. (2024, June 19). *Stress symptoms.* WebMD. https://www.webmd.com/balance/stress-management/stress-symptoms-effects_of-stress-on-the-body

Neff, K. (2024). *What is Self-Compassion?* Self Compassion. https://self-compassion.org/what-is-self-compassion/

Quote by Mahatma Gandhi. (n.d). Quotation. https://quotation.io/quote/way-peace-peace

Sander, L. (2019, January 25). *What does clutter do to your brain and body?* NewsGP. https://www1.racgp.org.au/newsgp/clinical/what-does-clutter-do-to-your-brain-and-body

We can never obtain peace in the outer world until we make peace with ourselves. (n.d.) Brainy Quote. https://www.brainyquote.com/quotes/dalai_lama_385012

Printed in Great Britain
by Amazon